Introduction

Welcome to *Non-Fiction To 14*. We know from talking to lots of English teachers that you have been wanting a resource that helps build students' understanding of a wider range of texts – in particular, non-fiction texts. Well, here it is.

In putting *Non-Fiction To 14* together, we wanted to achieve a number of aims. First, we wanted to serve up an eclectic range of new writing, genres and styles that would surprise and entertain students. You'll find an extraordinary variety of sources here including essays, letters, reviews, blogs, speeches, journal entries, newspaper and magazine articles, biography, travel writing and guides all of which have been carefully selected to interest and engage students.

We also wanted to give provide a rich range of texts written across different time periods because we know that students need to build their confidence with the language and stylistic conventions of 19th- and 20th-century texts. This is also an essential way of building students' reading resilience, that ability to enjoy rather than be scared of encountering the unfamiliar.

The activities throughout the book have been written to develop the skills students need to read and respond to non-fiction texts, from comprehension skills to analysing how language and structure can be used to convey meaning and create deliberate effects. Additional activities help students make comparisons across and between texts, further developing their critical reading skills.

As well as developing students' skills as critical readers of non-fiction texts, specific activities are designed to nurture their abilities as writers, enabling them to draw on the techniques they have explored in their reading when writing themselves.

We're proud to have produced a textbook so rich in new material. It will serve as a great foundation for students as they move on in their English studies. But we also see this as a fully-fledged collection of texts in its own right, offering students insights, surprises, bold new views of the world, and all the other experiences that great English lessons have always provided.

I hope you enjoy using it, and that your students enjoy working from it.

Geoff Barton

Contents

NO   ION

14

GEOFF BARTON
CHRISTOPHER EDGE

OXFORD
UNIVERSITY PRESS

OXFORD
UNIVERSITY PRESS

Great Clarendon Street, Oxford, OX2 6DP, United Kingdom

Oxford University Press is a department of the University of Oxford. It furthers the University's objective of excellence in research, scholarship, and education by publishing worldwide. Oxford is a registered trade mark of Oxford University Press in the UK and in certain other countries

Introduction © Geoff Barton 2018
Text © Oxford University Press 2018

The moral rights of the author have been asserted

First published in 2018

British Library Cataloguing in Publication Data

Data available

ISBN 978-019-837683-5

10 9 8 7 6 5 4 3 2 1

Printed in Great Britain by Bell and Bain Ltd., Glasgow

Acknowledgements

The author and publisher are grateful for permission to reprint extracts from the following copyright material:

Tanya Basu: 'Something called "attention residue" is ruining your concentration', *New York Magazine* - 'Science of Us', 21 Jan 2016, reprinted by permission of New York Media.

Luke Brown: 'The kitesurfer who defied a coma', *Daily Telegraph*, 26 April 2016, copyright © Telegraph Media Group Ltd 2016, reprinted by permission of TMG.

Roger Callan: 'Would you like to sit on the floor?', *The Independent*, 7 April 1999, copyright © The Independent 1999, reprinted by permission of Independent Print Ltd/ ESI Media.

Richard Feynman: *Surely You're Joking Mr Feynman: adventures of a curious character as told to Ralph Leighton* (Vintage 1992), copyright © Richard Feynman 1985, 1992, reprinted by permission of The Random House Group Ltd

Josh Gardner: 'Hotel unveils ROBOT butler that makes automated room service calls and accepts reviews from guests instead of tips' *Mailonline*, 12 Aug 2014, copyright © Associated Newspapers Ltd 2014, reprinted by permission of Solo Syndication

The Guardian Archive: Review - Theatre Royal *Richard III*, 3 Sept 1825; 'Londoners skate on thin ice', 23 Dec 1864; and 'The servantless house', 28 Dec 1921; copyright © Guardian News & Media Ltd 2017, reprinted by permission of GNM.

James Harrison: 'The Foodbank dilemma', *New Statesman*, October 2014, copyright © New Statesman 2014, reprinted by permission of New Statesman.

C S Lewis: Letter to Joan Lancaster, 1956, from *C S Lewis' Letters to Children* (Collins, 1985, copyright © C S Lewis Pte Ltd 1985, reprinted by permission of The C S Lewis Company Ltd.

Alyson Lynch: 'Penguin swims 5000 miles every year for reunion with man who saved his life', *Metro*, 9 March 2016, copyright © Associated Newspapers Ltd 2016, reprinted by permission of Solo Syndication.

Robert Macfarlane: *The Old Ways: a journey on foot* (Penguin, 2013), copyright © Robert Macfarlane 2013, reprinted by permission of Penguin Books Ltd.

George Orwell: *Down and Out in Paris and London* (Penguin, 2013), copyright © George Orwell 1933, reprinted by permission of A M Heath & Co Ltd, on behalf of the Estate of George Orwell.

Sue Townsend: 'A Passion for Books', copyright © Sue Townsend 1992, in *The Pleasure of Reading* edited by Antonia Fraser (Bloomsbury, 1992), reprinted by permission of Curtis Brown Group Ltd, London on behalf of the Estate of Sue Townsend

Peter Travers: Review of William Shakespeare's *Romeo and Juliet, Rolling Stone Magazine*, 1 Nov 1996, copyright © Rolling Stone LLC 1996, reprinted by permission of Rolling Stone LLC. All rights reserved.

Alfred Wainwright: *The Southern Fells* (Frances Lincoln, 2005), *Pictorial Guides to the Lakelands*, Book 4, copyright © The Estate of A Wainright 1960, reprinted by permission of Frances Lincoln Ltd, Quarto Publishing plc.

David Walliams: 'Roald Dahl and Me', *The Independent*, 4 Nov 2009, copyright © The Independent 2009, reprinted by permission of Independent Print Ltd/ ESI Media.

Jacqueline Wilson: 'Top Tips for Creative Writing', 17 March 2017, W H Smith blog, reprinted by permission of David Higham Associates.

Although we have made every effort to trace and contact all copyright holders before publication this has not been possible in all cases. If notified, the publisher will rectify any errors or omissions at the earliest opportunity.

The publisher and authors would like to thank the following for permission to use photographs and other copyright material:

Cover: sharpstock/Alamy Stock Photo; Vera Holera/Shutterstock; **p13:** Michal Vitek/Shutterstock; **p14-15:** Dan Baciu/Shutterstock; **p16:** Roman Levenko/Shutterstock; **p19:** Granger Historical Picture Archive/Alamy Stock Photo; **p20:** Old Paper Studios/Alamy Stock Photo; **p21:** Chronicle/ Alamy Stock Photo; **p24:** ne2pi/Shutterstock; **p27:** Sarah2/Shutterstock; **p29:** fizkes/Shutterstock; **p30:** Hirarchivum Press/Alamy Stock Photo; **p31:** Historical image collection by Bildagentur-online/Alamy Stock Photo; **p32-33:** cornfield/Shutterstock; **p37:** Ben Molyneux/Alamy Stock Photo; **p39:** Featureflash Photo Agency/Shutterstock; **p41:** CBW/Alamy Stock Photo; **p43:** Pictorial Press Ltd/Alamy Stock Photo; **p44-45:** olaser/iStockphoto; **p46, 48:** Chronicle/Alamy Stock Photo; **p50:** vipman/Shutterstock; **p52:** Zapp2Photo/Shutterstock; **p54:** Wolverhampton City Council - Arts and Heritage/Alamy Stock Photo; **p55:** Credit line Granger Historical Picture Archive/Alamy Stock Photo; **p56:** hronicle/Alamy Stock Photo; **p59:** Aila Images/Shutterstock; **p60:** Steven Lee/Alamy Stock Photo; **p63:** Thinglass/ Shutterstock; **p67:** Stephen Barnes/Alamy Stock Photo; **p69:** traveler1116/ iStockphoto; **p71:** JATUPHONG KRONGTHANIN/Shutterstock; **p72:** Stephen_Hikida/Shutterstock; **p75:** olga_gl/Shutterstock; **p77:** Dereje/ Shutterstock; **p78:** Boitano Photography/Alamy Stock Photo; **p79:** David Osborn/Shutterstock; **p81:** Line Icons by freebird/Shutterstock; **p82:** angellodeco/Shutterstock; **p84:** Science History Images/Alamy Stock Photo; **p85:** INTERFOTO/Alamy Stock Photo; **p87,88:** Everett Collection Historical/Alamy Stock Photo; **p89:** sdecoret/Shutterstock; **p94:** Galyna Andrushko/Shutterstock; **p96-97:** Michael Conrad/Shutterstock; **p98:** dabjola/Shutterstock; p99: CBW/Alamy Stock Photo; **p101:** Bhandol/Alamy Stock Photo; **p104:** Christopher Mills/Alamy Stock Photo; **p107:** mrtom-uk/ iStockphoto; **p109:** Chronicle/Alamy Stock Photo; **p111:** Archive Pics/Alamy Stock Photo; **p114:** lafoto/Shutterstock; **p115:** Universal History Archive/ Getty Images; **p116-117:** 135pixels/Shutterstock; **p118:** Allsorts Stock Photo/Alamy Stock Photo; **p123:** ken biggs/Alamy Stock Photo; **p126:** eye35. pix/Alamy Stock Photo; **p127:** Pictorial Press Ltd/Alamy Stock Photo; **p131:** Heritage Image Partnership Ltd/Alamy Stock Photo; **p133:** duncan1890/ iStockphoto; **p134:** Carmen Murillo/Shutterstock.

Every effort has been made to contact copyright holders of material reproduced in this book. Any omissions will be rectified in subsequent printings if notice is given to the publisher.

How to use this book

Structure

The structure of *Non-fiction to 14* is straightforward: each chapter focuses on one non-fiction text from the 19th century, one from the 20th century and another from the 21st century, all linked by theme. Each chapter is designed to support students as they develop their reading and writing skills, with the level of challenge increasing as students work through the chapter, as well as increasing progressively through the book as a whole.

Big picture

Each chapter begins with a 'Big picture' section to introduce the common theme of the non-fiction texts. It asks a question for students to consider, to relate the theme of the chapter to their own experiences and ideas.

Skills

Non-fiction to 14 has been designed to develop a range of reading and writing skills:

- Understand the meaning of a text
- Make inferences and refer to evidence in a text
- Comment on a writer's use of language
- Comment on a writer's use of structure
- Compare texts
- Practise writing different genres of non-fiction, drawing on techniques explored in reading

These skills move from the more literal requirements of reading, such as basic comprehension, to the higher-level skills of critical reading, including comparing texts and exploring how information, concepts and views are created and conveyed. In addition to this, students will develop their skills in writing non-fiction, drawing on the techniques explored in their reading.

Before reading

The 'Before reading' activities will activate students' prior knowledge of the themes and issues explored in the three non-fiction texts. They will contextualize the reading to follow.

Source texts

Each chapter includes three non-fiction texts or extracts, from three different centuries. These high-quality extracts have been chosen to illustrate a broad spectrum of non-fiction text types. The aim is not only to help students recognize key aspects of effective presentation of content, but also to encourage them to broaden their wider reading.

Each text is preceded by a short introduction, designed to help students understand the source of the text and the context for the extract they are about to read. In this introduction, students will also be asked a question to help them to engage more actively with the text that follows. This question can be set as a reading task, but many are also designed for discussion because high-quality talk feeds high-quality reading and writing.

Basic and advanced reading questions

The questions that follow each text are divided into 'basic' and 'advanced' reading questions. The basic questions generally expect decoding and comprehension. The advanced questions require students to explore language and structural features, making judgements about presentation and effectiveness.

Extended reading and writing activities

Each chapter ends with two extended assignments: an extended reading activity and an extended writing activity. These extended activities are designed to develop the skills explored in greater detail, sometimes asking students to orchestrate a range of skills in their responses.

Early bird

The 'Early bird' feature at the end of each chapter is designed to provide students who complete their reading and writing activities with a quirky challenge to keep them engaged. These 'Early bird' activities include word games, writing challenges and puzzles, and aim to reward students who have completed a task in a motivating way.

Source texts and writing tasks

Source texts: type of non-fiction

	Chapter 1	Chapter 2	Chapter 3	Chapter 4	Chapter 5	Chapter 6	Chapter 7	Chapter 8	Chapter 9	Chapter 10
Newspaper article	✓✓	✓	✓	✓✓		✓				
Magazine article			✓				✓		✓✓	
Speech							✓			
Journal								✓		
Review										✓✓
Blog		✓			✓					✓
Essay			✓			✓				
Eyewitness account						✓				
Guide		✓		✓				✓		
Autobio-graphical	✓						✓		✓	
Letter					✓					
Biography					✓					
Travel writing								✓		

Writing tasks: type of non-fiction

	Chapter 1	Chapter 2	Chapter 3	Chapter 4	Chapter 5	Chapter 6	Chapter 7	Chapter 8	Chapter 9	Chapter 10
Newspaper article	✓			✓						
Speech							✓			
Journal								✓		
Review										✓
Blog									✓	
Essay			✓							
Eyewitness account						✓				
Guidebook		✓								
Letter					✓					

Exploring language and structural features

When you read and respond to a non-fiction text, you might be asked to explore a writer's use of language or structure. Look at the tables below to remind yourself of some of the features of language and structure you could look out for.

Remember that as well as identifying these different features in a text, you need to be able to explain the effects that they create.

Exploring language

Look at the table below to remind yourself of some of the most common grammatical features used at word and phrase level.

Grammatical feature	Definition	Example
Noun	A word used to name a person, place or thing	The *pen* is mightier than the *sword*. The *danger* is *overconfidence*.
Adjective	A word which describes a noun	It was a *jagged* cliff. The weather grew *cold*.
Verb	A word that identifies actions, thoughts, feelings or the state of being	I *believe* this is true. She *shouts* at me to stop. *Leave* him alone.
Tense	The tense of the verb tells you when the action of the verb takes place (present, past or future)	I *am washing* the car now. I *washed* the car yesterday. I *will wash* the car tomorrow.
Adverb	A word that adds meaning to a verb, adjective or another adverb	It was *strangely* quiet. *Sometimes* we have pizza for tea, We looked *everywhere*.
Adverbial	A group of words that function as an adverb	He worked *very hard*. The dog slept *under the table*.
Noun phrase	A group of words that has a noun as its head, or key word. All the words in the group tell us more about the head noun.	A *big muddy puddle*
Prepositional phrase	A word or phrase used with a noun or pronoun to show place, position, time or means.	In a moment, far beneath.

Now look at the table below to remind yourself of some of the most common literary techniques.

Literary technique	Definition	Example
Alliteration	The repetition of the same letter or sound at the beginning of a group of words for special effect	Drab and depressing
Dialogue	Words spoken by characters in a play, film or story	'I can't work it out, can you?' 'No, this kind of device was never my strong point,' Jake replied.
Emotive language	Words and phrases that arouse emotion	This wasn't death; this was murder.
Hyperbole	A deliberately exaggerated statement that is not meant to be taken literally	He was the size of an elephant.
Imagery/descriptive detail	Writing which creates a picture or appeals to other senses – this includes simile, metaphor and personification and the use of vivid verbs, nouns, adjectives and adverbs	We knew the house smelt fusty and dank but we didn't expect the lacy cobwebs and the oozing walls.
Metaphor	The use of a word or phrase which describes something by likening it to something else	He was a monkey in class.
Onomatopoeia	Words which imitate the sound they represent	Buzz, pop, crackle
Personification	A form of metaphor whereby an inanimate object is given the qualities of a living being	The rocks reached for the sky.
Repetition	Words or phrases which are repeated for effect	She ran, ran for her life.
Rhetorical question	A question asked for dramatic effect and not intended to get an answer.	But how do we know this is the case?
Simile	A comparison where one thing is compared to another using the words *like* or *as*.	He was as quiet as a mouse.
Tricolon (pattern of three)	Groups of three related words or phrases placed close together	The paint was peeling, the windows were cracked and the floorboards were rotting.

Exploring structural features

Structural features can include sentence forms a writer uses, for example, the sentence types (statement, question, command, exclamation) and sentence structures (single and multi-clause sentences) used.

Look at the table below to remind yourself of some of the most common structural features at sentence level.

Structural feature	Explanation	Example
Clause	Part of a sentence with its own verb	After she ran down the road
Simple sentence (single clause sentence)	The most basic type of sentence consisting of a subject and a verb	The girl stood.
Compound sentence (a type of multi-clause sentence)	A sentence containing two independent clauses linked by a coordinating conjunction	The dog ate his dinner but I had nothing.
Complex sentence (a type of multi-clause sentence)	A sentence containing a main clause and one or more subordinate clauses linked by a subordinating conjunction such as *because*, *as*, *although* or a relative pronoun such as *who*, *that* or *which*	The boy, who lived next door to me, was older than I was.

When you look at the structure of the text, you should also explore the following aspects:

- the sequence through the text, that is, how the text is organized
- the focus of a text, that is, where the writer is directing the reader's attention
- the coherence of a text, that is, the connections made between ideas, themes and paragraphs
- evidence of viewpoint and counter viewpoint
- evidence of bias
- links between the opening and ending of a text
- the balance between dialogue, description and action.

Adventurous or reckless?

Source texts table

Texts	Genre	Date
1.1 'The kitesurfer who defied a coma' by Luke Brown	Newspaper article	2016
1.2 'Flying the English Channel' by Harriet Quimby	Autobiographical account	1912
1.3 'Londoners skate on thin ice' (Anonymous)	Newspaper article	1874

Big picture

Lots of people enjoy dangerous pursuits, from extreme sports such as kitesurfing and speed skating, to adventurous exploits such as crossing the oceans in one-person vehicles. The question is, should people be allowed to take part in activities that could injure or kill them? Are they being adventurous or just reckless?

In this chapter you will read three non-fiction texts about people who take part in risky pursuits: a newspaper article about a champion kitesurfer; an autobiographical account written by the first woman to fly across the English Channel; and a newspaper article describing how some Londoners risked their lives by skating on frozen lakes.

Skills

- Understand the meaning of a text

- Make inferences and refer to evidence in a text

- Comment on a writer's use of language and structure (including **sentence forms**, quotations and powerful openings)

- Compare texts

- Practise writing a newspaper article, drawing on techniques and ideas explored in reading

Key term

Sentence forms sentence types (that is, statement, question, command, exclamation) and sentence structures (that is, simple, minor, multi-clause)

Before reading

1   Look at the list of extreme sports on page 13. They have been sorted into groups.

a   Firstly, read through the groups to see which sports you know and which are new to you.

b   Where there are sports you have never heard of, look closely at each word and try to work out what you think the activity consists of. Write down your idea and explain how you came up with your suggestion.

c Choose five extreme sports from the overall list. Write them down in order of *most* dangerous to *least* dangerous. Compare your list with a friend's.

Earth:
skateboarding, longboarding, mountain boarding, sandboarding, drifting, BMX, motocross, FMX, aggressive inline skating, mountain biking, caving, abseiling, rock climbing, free climbing, bouldering, mountaineering, parkour, sand kiting, zorbing

Water:
surfing, long/short body boarding, water-skiing, wakeboarding, kitesurfing, windsurfing, cave diving, flowboarding, paddle surfing/stand up paddle, kayaking, cliff jumping, coasteering, scuba diving, knee boarding, white water rafting, skim boarding, jet-skiing

Snow and ice:
snowboarding, snow skiing, ice climbing, snowmobiling, snow kiting

Air:
base jumping, sky-diving, wing suiting, bungee jumping, high-lining, hang-gliding, paragliding, slacklining

2 Some extreme sports involve real risks to the people taking part. They also create worry for the person's family. Think of two reasons why people might like to take part in extreme sports, even though they put themselves at risk.

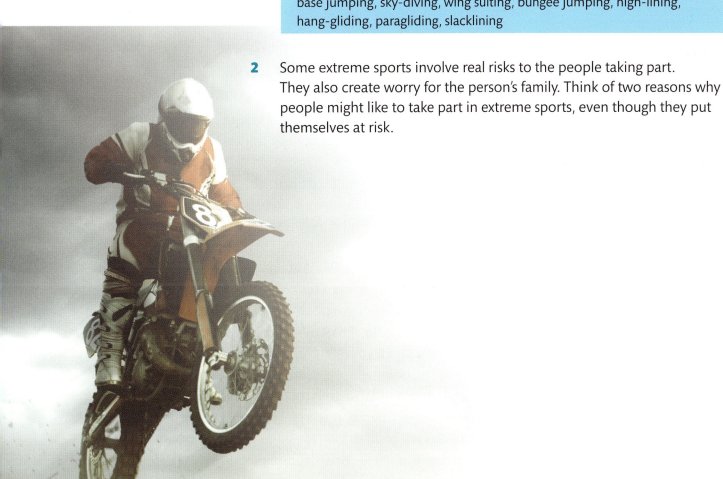

1.1 'The kitesurfer who defied a coma' by Luke Brown, 2016

The following newspaper article is about the champion kitesurfer Lewis Crathern and was first published in the *Daily Telegraph* on 26 April 2016. The article describes someone who takes on dangerous challenges around the world. As you read the text, decide whether you think that Lewis Crathern is brave or reckless. What do you think the writer's attitude towards him seems to be?

Source text 1.1

WORD BANK

conviction certainty

formidable major

induced coma being made unconscious deliberately by doctors as part of treatment

befitting of appropriate for

G force the force acting on a person or object as a result of acceleration

"Kitesurfing is an extremely safe sport," says Lewis Crathern, and, for a moment, you could be forgiven for thinking he is joking. The words, despite the **conviction** with which they are spoken, sound strange coming from his mouth. Because, less than three months ago, 5 a **formidable** crash out on the water left Crathern in an **induced coma**, in a lonely South African hospital bed, fighting for his life.

During the semi-finals of the Red Bull King of the Air competition in Blouberg, Crathern had attempted to execute a routine kite loop in an attempt to impress the watching judges. But the move went wrong. 10 His kite stalled, and Crathern knocked himself unconscious on his own board, before falling twenty feet into the water. He was in a coma for almost a week, with doctors initially predicting he would be in hospital for over a month.

Fast-forward six weeks, and the Worthing-based kitesurfer is back 15 to wowing the crowds off the picture-postcard coast of El Gouna, Egypt in the first leg on the 2016 World Kite Tour calendar. "I suppose it is quite soon," he says in gloriously understated fashion, when asked about the pace of his recovery.

"But it is important in life to always keep moving. I spent six days 20 in a coma after the accident, and after that I spent another four weeks doing absolutely nothing, which was hell for me. I like to be doing things, and I desperately didn't want to miss the first event in Egypt. And, in the end, I felt just about fit enough to fly there."

Crathern is speaking from his current location in the French Alps, 25 which he is travelling through to compete in the second leg of the World Tour in Leucate; a globe-trotting international competition **befitting of** a rapidly developing sport. "It's nice to take in this kind of scenery," he comments, delighted to be back on the road.

Four weeks spent lazing on a sofa in front of Netflix was never 30 likely to sit well with a man whose lifestyle appears almost as extreme as the profession he lives for. As well as his formidable kitesurfing CV – Crathern was freestyle British champion from 2005 to 2008, and made headlines when he jumped over both Worthing and Brighton

35 piers – the 31-year-old is also one of the sport's biggest personalities back on dry land, working as both a commentator and public speaker.

That was all threatened in February, though, when Crathern's career was put on temporary hold after his attempted 'Mega Loop' stunt in South Africa went so disastrously wrong.

40 "A mega loop is a move where we loop the kite 360 degrees whilst we are high up in the air," he explains. "The **G force** is such that it is like being shot out of a cannon, and somehow I ended up falling backwards onto my kite. A cat always lands on its feet and kitesurfers tend to always land forwards, but this time I got my head stuck backwards and I couldn't get out of it.

45 "My heels then caught on the rails of my board, and my head was whipped back against it, and I was immediately knocked out. But it was nothing more than an unlucky landing, and so there was never any thinking on my part of not getting involved again. To be honest what happened doesn't bother me all that much, and there is

50 certainly no damage there mentally."

Understandably, returning to the sport, and doing so with such little recovery time, meant **allaying** the concerns of his nearest and dearest – "it is amazing how much I've seen [the crash] affect my family and friends," he **concedes** – as well as returning to elite level

55 competition in less than ideal physical condition.

But as well as the short-term desire to compete in Egypt ("a country where kiteboarding is booming because of the perfect conditions it offers learners, and an ideal place to have a stop of the world tour in"), Crathern also found himself motivated by something of a bigger picture.

60 A keen kitesurfing commentator, he enjoys nothing more than coaxing new participants into trying out the extreme sport, which brings us back to his somewhat surprising insistence that his is a safe sport.

"Honestly, I am **adamant** that it is a completely safe sport," he **pointedly reiterates**. "Obviously accidents happen, but they also happen

65 when you are driving a vehicle, or when you cross the road. Whenever you push the envelope of a sport, the risks are always going to be higher.

"For beginners, it is a very safe sport, and I often say to people on my commentary 'why not give it a go?' Safety releases have improved so much over the past five years, and the introduction that people receive in the

70 sport these days is light-years ahead of what we had ten years ago. It is very accessible, and ultimately there are so many people kitesurfing who wouldn't dream of participating in another extreme sport, which is great."

WORD BANK

allaying calming

concedes accepts

adamant certain

pointedly sharply

reiterates repeats

Basic reading skills

1 Look again at the opening paragraph of the article. Write down three **facts** we learn about Lewis Crathern.

2 In the second paragraph, the writer explains what led to Lewis Crathern's accident. He says he was attempting a 'routine kite loop'. What does the word 'routine' mean in this context?

3 Look at the third paragraph. Lewis Crathern is competing 'off the picture-postcard coast of El Gouna'. Which of the terms below is closest in meaning to 'picture-postcard'? Write it down and explain your answer in a sentence:

unreal

tacky

artificial

beautiful

far from home

4 As well as being a successful kitesurfer, what two roles is Lewis Crathern known for back home?

5 Why is Egypt popular with kitesurfers?

6 At the start and end of the article, Lewis Crathern says that kitesurfing is a safe sport. Write down one reason that he gives.

Key term

facts things that are known to have happened or be true

Advanced reading skills

1 Look at the opening sentence. How does the writer draw the reader into the article?

2 Throughout the article the writer refers to his subject as 'Crathern', not as 'Lewis Crathern' or just 'Lewis'. In your own words explain what effect this has and how the article would be different if the writer used the first name Lewis throughout.

3 In the third paragraph the writer uses the phrase 'gloriously understated fashion'. Explain what you think 'gloriously' means in this context.

4 In the sixth paragraph, the writer describes Crathern as 'a man whose lifestyle appears almost as extreme as the profession he lives for'. In your own words, explain what you think he means.

5 In the ninth paragraph, Lewis Crathern describes the accident he had in South Africa. Choose two words from the options below that you think best describe his attitude. Explain your choices.

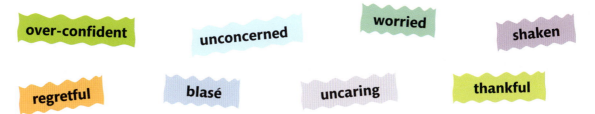

over-confident   unconcerned   worried   shaken

regretful   blasé   uncaring   thankful

6 How does the writer present Lewis Crathern? Does he seem to view him completely as a hero, or does he seem to have some criticisms of him? Write a paragraph in which you discuss the way the subject is presented.

You might comment on:

■ the details the writer gives about Crathern's background and achievements

■ the way he uses quotations

■ the labels he uses to describe his subject

■ the choice of words he uses to hint at his own opinions (for example, 'understandably', 'pointedly', 'adamant')

■ the impact on his family

■ his views about safety developments.

1.2 'Flying the English Channel' by Harriet Quimby, 1912

The following autobiographical account is by one of the world's first aviators – Harriet Quimby. In the early days of aeroplanes, the machines were rickety, unreliable and often dangerous. They were made from wood and canvas held together with piano wire. In view of this, what sort of qualities do you think early pilots needed?

Harriet Quimby arrived in New York City in 1903, landing a job as a reporter. She met a flying instructor and asked him to teach her to fly. She showed exceptional skills and in August 1911 became the first American woman to gain a pilot's licence.

In 1912 Harriet Quimby attempted to fly the English Channel in exchange for exclusive coverage by the *Daily Mirror* newspaper. It was the first attempt made by a woman. She made her flight in the early morning hours of 16 April 1912, taking off from Dover. This is her account of her flight.

Source text 1.2

WORD BANK

preliminaries
preparations

vantage viewpoint

flagstaff flagpole

moving-picture men
film-makers

jiffy a very short time

It was five-thirty A.M. when my machine got off the ground. The **preliminaries** were brief. Hearty handshakes were quickly given, the motor began to make its twelve hundred revolutions a minute, and I put up my hand to give the signal of release. Then I was off. The

5 noise of the motor drowned the shouts and cheers of friends below. In a moment I was in the air, climbing steadily in a long circle. I was up fifteen hundred feet within thirty seconds. From this high point of **vantage** my eyes lit at once on Dover Castle. It was half hidden in a fog bank. I felt that trouble was coming, but I made directly for

10 the **flagstaff** of the castle, as I had promised the waiting *Mirror* photographers and the **moving-picture men** I should do.

In an instant I was beyond the cliffs and over the channel. Far beneath I saw the *Mirror's* tug, with its stream of black smoke. It was trying to keep ahead of me, but I passed it in a **jiffy**. Then the

15 quickening fog obscured my view. Calais was out of sight. I could not see ahead of me or at all below. There was only one thing for me to do and that was to keep my eyes fixed on my compass.

My hands were covered with long Scotch woolen gloves which gave me good protection from the cold and fog; but the machine was wet and

20 my face was so covered with dampness that I had to push my goggles up on my forehead. I could not see through them. I was traveling at over a mile a minute. The distance straight across from Dover to Calais is only twenty-five miles, and I knew that land must be in sight if I could only get below the fog and see it. So I dropped from an altitude of about two

25 thousand feet until I was half that height. The sunlight struck upon my

1. Adventurous or reckless?

WORD BANK

reconnoiter survey/
   explore

alight land

face and my eyes lit upon the white and sandy shores of France. I felt happy, but could not find Calais. Being unfamiliar with the coast line, I could not locate myself. I determined to **reconnoiter** and come down to a height of about five hundred feet and traverse the shore.

30   Meanwhile, the wind had risen and the currents were coming in billowy gusts. I flew a short distance inland to locate myself or find a good place on which to **alight**. It was all tilled land below me, and rather than tear up the farmers' fields I decided to drop down on the hard and sandy beach. I did so at once, making an easy landing. Then

35   I jumped from my machine and was alone upon the shore. But it was only for a few moments. A crowd of fishermen – men, women and children each carrying a pail of sand worms – came rushing from all directions toward me. They were chattering in French, of which I comprehended sufficient to discover that they knew I had crossed the

40   channel. These humble fisherfolk knew what had happened. They were congratulating themselves that the first woman to cross in an aeroplane had landed on their fishing beach.

Basic reading skills

1a   Re-read the opening paragraph. At what time does Harriet Quimby take off?

1b   How long does it take Harriet Quimby to reach a height of 1500 feet?

1c   What landmark has Harriet Quimby promised the photographers she would fly towards after take-off?

2a   What are the weather conditions like during Harriet Quimby's crossing of the channel? Pick out two quotations that you think best show this.

2b   List two actions that Harriet Quimby takes to cope with the effects of the weather conditions.

3   Name the two places where Harriet Quimby could land when she reaches France. Explain which one she chooses and why.

4   Who are the first people to know that Harriet Quimby has successfully crossed the English Channel?

19

Advanced reading skills

Key term

prepositional phrase
a word or phrase used with a noun or pronoun to show place, position, time or means, for example, *in a moment, far beneath*

1. How does the writer's use of **prepositional phrases** help the reader to share her experience?

2. Re-read the paragraph beginning: 'My hands were covered with long Scotch woolen gloves...' Comment on how the writer's use of sentence forms conveys Harriet Quimby's feelings and actions. You should comment on the effects created by the variety of sentence types, for example, single and multi-clause.

3. Compare this autobiographical account with the newspaper article on pages 14–15. What impression do you get of Harriet Quimby's and Lewis Crathern's achievements? In your answer you should comment on:

   ■ what you learn about each person and how this information is presented

   ■ what you admire about their achievements

   ■ any concerns or doubts you have about their attitudes and actions, and the reasons for these.

1.3 'Londoners skate on thin ice', 1874

The following article, first published in *The Guardian* newspaper on 23 December 1874, describes how some Londoners have been skating on frozen lakes in the city's parks. As you read, think about how risky the writer makes this activity sound.

Source text 1.3

WORD BANK

notwithstanding in spite of

immersions the action of putting someone or something in a liquid

Notwithstanding the dangerous state of the ice on the waters in the London parks on Monday, a considerable number of persons ventured upon it during the day, and many of them had narrow escapes from drowning.

5   On the Long Water in Kensington Gardens about 1,500 sliders and skaters went on the ice, and thirty fell in. About midday the ice gave way in the centre, in deep water, and four men were for several minutes in great danger, but were rescued by William Hemmings, the iceman, at the risk of his own life. In the Regent's Park about

10 2,000 persons were on the lake during the day, and there were twenty **immersions**. In St James's Park about 2,000 persons, chiefly boys, went on the ice during the day, and there were thirty immersions.

    About nine o'clock on Monday night four young men and two young women belonging to the establishment of Messrs. Swan and

15 Edgar, in Regent Street, who had formed themselves into a skating party, reached the **Serpentine**. One young man, a German, named S. Fierstadt, was determined to show his friends how secure the ice was before they ventured upon it, and was heard to remark, "I'll put on my skates and prove it all right." It unfortunately happened that

20 huge blocks of ice had drifted from the bridge and rested near the shore. Upon this the young man skated until he came to the middle of the water, where there was only thin rotten ice. Here he at once disappeared, giving a great plunge into the water.

His friends' cries for help were **appalling**. In one minute a fine

25 young fellow, George Talbolt Cobbett, a builder, took his coat off and plunged in after the drowning man. He was shortly joined by three other swimmers, named Daniel Pinkerton, George Wolverton, and James Wilson, but as the ice was now broken into large square pieces it continually baffled them, and their efforts were futile.

30 Meanwhile some of the drowning man's friends had given information to the Royal Humane Society's receiving-house, and under the instruction of Mr. Superintendent Williams, Mr John Parsons, chief boatman, Mr John Winnett. And another Serpentine waterman put on their lifebelts, slung the boat from the shed into

35 the road, and drew it down the slippery pathway to the scene of the accident, with the assistance of Police Sergeant Osborne and others.

The boat was then pushed over the broken ice to the spot where the man had fallen in, and by the aid of a long pole and drat, the lifeless body was drawn out of the water, having been under the ice more

40 than a quarter of an hour.

After this another tragical scene occurred; the men who had been swimming in the water all became **prostrate** with the cold, and were carried by the spectators to the receiving-house, where they were placed in warm baths and given stimulants, which ultimately revived them.

WORD BANK

Serpentine a lake in Hyde Park, London

appalling shocking, very unpleasant

prostrate lying face downwards

Basic reading skills

1a How many people fell into the water when skating on the frozen lake in Regent's Park?

1b How many people in total does the writer say went skating on the Long Water in Kensington Gardens?

1c Were the people who went skating in St James's Park mainly male or female?

2 What was the young man who drowned in the Serpentine heard to say before he went skating on the lake?

3a Pick out a quotation that shows the first attempt to rescue the man drowning in the Serpentine was unsuccessful.

3b Explain your choice of quotation, commenting on any specific words that convey the failure of the rescue attempt.

4 The writer begins the final paragraph: 'After this another tragical scene occurred...'. Explain whether you agree that the scene described in this paragraph is a 'tragical' one. Give reasons for your answer.

Advanced reading skills

Key terms

verb a word that identifies actions, thoughts, feelings or the state of being

adverb a word that adds to the meaning of a verb, adjective or another adverb

adjective a word that describes a noun

1 How does the writer convey the risk of skating on London's frozen lakes? Think about:

- how the actions of the skaters are described
- the impression you get of the writer's attitude towards the skaters and how this is conveyed.

2 Look again at the three paragraphs describing the rescue of the drowning man from the Serpentine, beginning 'His friends' cries for help were appalling...'

How does the writer's use of language help to build tension in this section? In your answer you should comment on the effects created by:

- the writer's choices of vocabulary and descriptive details
- the writer's choices of **verbs**, **adverbs** and **adjectives**
- the writer's use of sentence forms.

3 Read what the following student has written about this text:

I think if this newspaper article was written today it would be a lot more sensationalized.

Explain what you think this student means and then say whether you agree or disagree with the statement. Give reasons for your answer.

Extended reading

Revisit the two newspaper articles you have read in this section, 'The kitesurfer who defied a coma' and 'Londoners skate on thin ice', in order to answer the following question.

Compare how the two writers use language to convey their attitude towards the subjects of their articles. In your answer you should:

- identify the writer's attitude in both texts
- compare the language choices each writer makes
- explore how these help to convey their attitude
- support your ideas with references to both texts.

Extended writing

Write a newspaper article reporting on Harriet Quimby's successful crossing of the English Channel. You should draw on information from the autobiographical account you have read on pages 18–19 and the techniques you have explored in the newspaper articles you have read in this section.

As you write, think about:

- how the opening of your article can hook the reader's attention
- how you can use language to suggest the magnitude of Harriet Quimby's achievement
- how you can link the ending of your article with the opening.

Remember to check the spelling, punctuation and grammar of your writing.

Early bird

Some people believe there should be an upper age limit on extreme sports. Write a blog in which you argue for or against an upper age limit for a particular extreme sport (for example, kitesurfing, cave-diving, bungee jumping, snowboarding). You might include arguments about:

- fitness levels
- susceptibility to injury
- the effects of injuries
- individual entitlement to express oneself through action.

Source texts table

Texts	Genre	Date
2.1 'Something Called "Attention Residue" Is Ruining Your Concentration' by Tanya Basu	Blog	2016
2.2 *The Young Woman's Book: A Useful Manual for Everyday Life* by Laura Valentine	Guide	1877
2.3 'Would you like to sit on the floor?' by Roger Callan	Newspaper article	1999

Big picture

The modern world is full of distractions. From the screens of our phones to the huge amount of information that surrounds us every day, we have to work hard to focus on the things we need to get done. How many times a day do you get distracted by social media?

In this section you will read three non-fiction texts that explore similar concerns: a blog post from an online magazine about the ability to concentrate in the 21st-century workplace; an extract from a 19th-century guide warning of the distractions that can be found in reading a novel; and a newspaper article from the end of the 20th century about different styles of learning and how schools should accommodate these.

Skills

- Understand the meaning of a text
- Make inferences and refer to evidence in a text
- Comment on a writer's use of language and structure (including level of formality, viewpoint, **hyperbole**, paragraphs and **rhetorical questions**)
- Explore the techniques used by a writer to communicate views and ideas
- Practise writing a guide, giving advice to other students, drawing on techniques and ideas explored in your reading

Before reading

Key terms

hyperbole a deliberately exaggerated statement that is not meant to be taken literally

rhetorical question a question asked for dramatic effect and not intended to get an answer

1   Think about your everyday life. What do you find distracts you from the things you want or need to get done, for example, text messages and social media?

2   If you have a task or project you have to concentrate on, do you have any strategies to stop yourself from getting distracted? Share your ideas.

3   Look at the following statements:

> **A.** It's better to focus on one task at a time in order to get more things done.

> **B.** If you can multitask and work on more than one thing at the same time you can be more productive.

Which statement do you most agree with? Give reasons for your answer.

4 Some researchers believe there are four types of learner:

- auditory learners – people who learn best by listening

- visual learners – people who learn best by reading and through pictures

- tactile learners – people who learn best through touch and making

- kinesthetic learners – people who learn best through physical activity.

What type of learner do you think you are? Can you think of an example of something that you have learned that demonstrates your preferred style of learning?

2.1 'Something Called "Attention Residue" Is Ruining Your Concentration' by Tanya Basu, 2016

The following text is a blog post written by the science journalist Tanya Basu, which was first published in *New York Magazine's* 'Science of Us' blog on 21 January 2016. Here she explores the phenomenon of 'attention residue' which is being blamed for people's inability to concentrate at work. As you read the blog, note down any times when you find yourself becoming distracted before you reach the end of the post.

Source text 2.1

WORD BANK

conundrum a riddle or difficult question

abstract a summary of the contents of a book, article or academic study

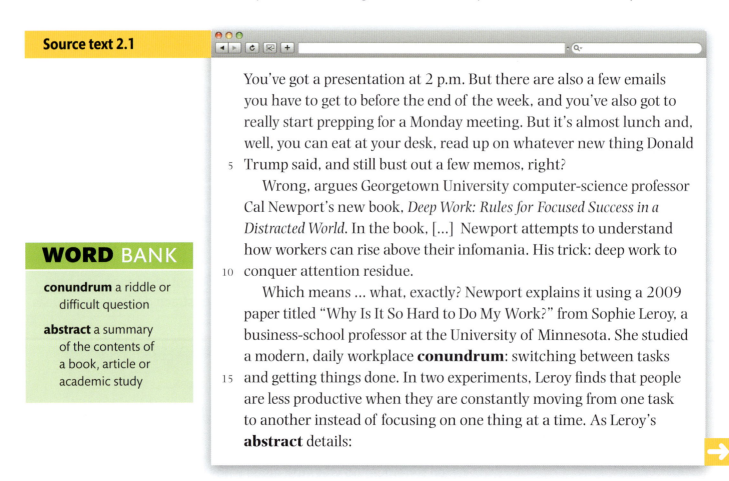

You've got a presentation at 2 p.m. But there are also a few emails you have to get to before the end of the week, and you've also got to really start prepping for a Monday meeting. But it's almost lunch and, well, you can eat at your desk, read up on whatever new thing Donald
5 Trump said, and still bust out a few memos, right?

Wrong, argues Georgetown University computer-science professor Cal Newport's new book, *Deep Work: Rules for Focused Success in a Distracted World*. In the book, [...] Newport attempts to understand how workers can rise above their infomania. His trick: deep work to
10 conquer attention residue.

Which means ... what, exactly? Newport explains it using a 2009 paper titled "Why Is It So Hard to Do My Work?" from Sophie Leroy, a business-school professor at the University of Minnesota. She studied a modern, daily workplace **conundrum**: switching between tasks
15 and getting things done. In two experiments, Leroy finds that people are less productive when they are constantly moving from one task to another instead of focusing on one thing at a time. As Leroy's **abstract** details:

WORD BANK

transition change from one task to another

20   "[P]eople need to stop thinking about one task in order to fully **transition** their attention and perform well on another. Yet, results indicate it is difficult for people to transition their attention away from an unfinished task and their subsequent task performance suffers."

    Leroy calls this carryover from one task to another "attention residue," where you're still thinking of a previous task as you start
25 another one. Even if you finish your task completely, you still have some attention residue swirling around your head as you embark on your next task, meaning that bullet point on your to-do list doesn't start off on the right foot. In other words, as much as multitasking gets nods for being an asset in today's time-crunched world, it's
30 not really a good thing when it comes to your productivity, and it's actually a time-waster.

    Here's where what Newport calls "deep work" comes in: He suggests focusing on a single, intense task for a long period of time to reach peak productivity. You don't get attention-residue issues, which
35 means your output is stronger, cleaner, and just plain better from a lack of distractions. So if you've got ten emails to write, block off some time to just focus on those emails. If you've got a presentation due tomorrow, put your away message on, sequester yourself, and focus on banging out that presentation. Most important: Don't stop — or
40 begin something else — until you're completely done.

Basic reading skills

1 Look again at the first paragraph. Give three examples of things that the writer lists as potential distractions.

2 What is the title of Professor Cal Newport's new book?

3 The writer states that Professor Newport's book 'attempts to understand how workers can rise above their infomania'.

   a Using information from the blog, provide definitions for the following terms:

   infomania

   attention residue

   time-crunched

   deep work

   b Using your words, explain what Professor Newport's book is trying to help workers to do.

4a Did Sophie Leroy's 2009 study find that people were more or less productive when switching between different tasks?

4b Using your own words, explain why Sophie Leroy thought this was.

5 Look again at the final paragraph. Summarize the advice this gives.

Advanced reading skills

1 A blog post is designed to be read online and has to compete for a reader's attention with other articles and tasks. How does the language that Tanya Basu uses help to attract and maintain the reader's attention? In your answer you should comment on:

   ■ the use of the **second person**, for example, 'You've got a presentation...'

   ■ her choice of **sentence forms**.

2 Look again at the paragraph beginning, '[P]eople need to stop thinking about one task...'

   a How formal is the register of language used here? Support your answer with reference to the text.

   b Does the informality of the language influence your response to the idea presented? Explain why.

Key terms

second person
addressing the reader as 'you'

sentence forms
sentence types (that is, statement, question, command, exclamation) and sentence structures (that is, simple, minor, multi-clause)

3 How does the structure of the blog post help Tanya Basu to present and explore the concept of 'attention residue' and how this can be overcome? Copy and complete the table to identify the focus of each paragraph.

Paragraph	Focus
1	Gives examples of some of the distractions found in a modern-day workplace, addressed directly to the reader.
2	Introduces the concept of 'attention residue' and...
3	
4	
5	
6	

Key term

counter viewpoint an opposing point of view

4 Tanya Basu creates links between paragraphs to help develop the ideas she presents and improve the coherence of the text.

For example, at the end of the first paragraph she asks a rhetorical question: '...still bust out a few memos, right?' and in the first sentence of the following paragraph immediately answers this in the negative: 'Wrong, argues...'. This allows the writer to challenge the idea she has just presented and introduce a **counter viewpoint**.

Find more examples of the links the writer creates between paragraphs and explore how these help her to develop ideas and improve the coherence of the text.

2.2 *The Young Woman's Book: A Useful Manual for Everyday Life* by Laura Valentine, 1877

The following extract is taken from a guide providing advice on etiquette for young women, first published in 1877. Here the writer warns of the dangerous distraction that reading a novel can be. As you read, think about how seriously the writer wants you to take this warning.

Source text 2.2

To sit over a foolish or even a *wise* novel when the daily duties of life demand our attention is absolutely *wicked*. We have seen, in our own life, the mother of a family devote herself to novel reading.

The father was at sea in the merchant service. A boy, a girl, and the
5 house demanded the wife's attention. The children were neglected, dirty, ragged, untaught, running about the roads; the house was dirty beyond description, for there was but one servant, who naturally, followed her mistress's example.

The wife could not make her income **suffice** her, because no one
10 watched against waste or dishonesty in the kitchen, and her husband, when he came home from sea, was arrested for her debts.

The son, utterly **ruined**, ran away from school, and finally disappeared in Australia. The daughter, trained only in the unreal **folly** of novels, married secretly a man much below her father's
15 station – he was also an **hereditary** madman!

When the mother of the boy and girl married, she had been a lovely, clever girl. But novel reading, like **intoxication**, brought misery on her and on two following generations.

WORD BANK

suffice to be enough for someone's needs

ruined damaged

folly a foolish action or idea

hereditary inherited, for example, a hereditary disease or characteristic is passed from one generation to the next

intoxication drunkenness

Basic reading skills

Key term

adjective a word that describes a noun

1a Look again at the first paragraph. What two **adjectives** does the writer use to describe a novel?

1b Pick out the quotation that you think best shows the writer's attitude to reading novels.

1c Summarize why the writer feels this way about reading novels.

2 List three pieces of evidence the writer gives that suggest the mother neglected her children.

3 What happened to the woman's husband when he came home from sea?

4 What happened to the woman's son?

5   Look again at the following sentence:

'The daughter, trained only in the unreal folly of novels, married secretly a man much below her father's station – he was also an hereditary madman!'

   a   Rewrite this sentence in your own words.

   b   Explain what the phrase 'unreal folly of novels' suggests about the writer's attitude to reading novels.

6   Now look at the final paragraph. What does the writer compare reading a novel to? Explain whether you think this is an appropriate comparison.

Advanced reading skills

Key terms

verb a word that identifies actions, thoughts, feelings or the state of being

adverb a word that adds to the meaning of a verb, adjective or another adverb

1   The writer uses hyperbole to present her view of the dangers of novel reading.

   a   Pick out any examples of hyperbole you can find in the text.

   b   How effective do you think the writer's use of hyperbole is? Give reasons for your answer.

2   How does the writer use emotive language to present her view of the dangers of novel reading? In your answer you should comment on the effects created by:

- the writer's choices of vocabulary and descriptive details
- the writer's choices of **verbs**, **adverbs** and adjectives
- the writer's use of exclamations and other sentence forms.

3a   The writer lists consequences which she connects to the mother's reading of novels. Copy and complete the table on below to record these consequences and give each one a danger rating (with 1 being the least dangerous and 5 the most dangerous).

Consequence	Danger rating
Not cleaning the house	1

3b   How has the writer structured her presentation of these consequences? What effect does this create?

4a   Look again at the opening and closing paragraphs of the extract. Explain any connections you can find between these.

4b   How effective do you think the closing paragraph is? Give reasons for your answer.

2.3 'Would you like to sit on the floor?' by Roger Callan, 1999

The following newspaper article was first published in the education section of *The Independent* newspaper on 7 April 1999. The writer presents researchers' findings about the way people learn and explores the effects this could have on the learning environment in schools at the end of the 20th century. As you read, think about whether the description of the classroom environment matches your own experience in school.

Source text 2.3

WORD BANK

prohibited banned

premium high value

initiatives strategies intended to resolve a difficulty or improve a situation

If you have visited Stratford-upon-Avon and entered the Grammar School that young Will Shakespeare attended, you will have seen his classroom. It is a regular classroom – wooden desks three abreast, in three rows, a big master's desk at the front. Nothing out of the
5 ordinary there. But that is the point: the classroom has not changed in 400 years! True, the teacher's cane has been **prohibited**, science labs have been introduced, and computers have made an appearance, but little else is new. Schools generally have hard chairs and desks, bright lights, silence, and teachers who talk much of the time. A **premium** is
10 therefore placed on the student who can sit still and silent for much of the school day, listening attentively. Such an environment suits some students perfectly, but it does not suit everyone.

Some learn better if they sit on something soft, or on the floor, whilst working, or have some music playing, or low lighting. Some
15 prefer to be doing several projects at once. Others like to eat while they work. For some, the environment doesn't matter.

Research has demonstrated that there are basically three types of learner: global, analytic and integrated. A global learner prefers the soft-seating, low-lighting, skipping-from-project-to-project approach.
20 An analytic learner prefers the hard seats and no distractions typified by a traditional classroom. The integrated or flexible learner is able to learn in a variety of different environments.

Within these groupings are four sub-groups – auditory (the person who learns best by listening), visual (learns best by reading and
25 through pictures), tactile (learns best through touch and making), kinesthetic (learns best using the whole body – through physical education or field trips).

These findings are based on more than 30 years of research into learning. Springing from a project commissioned in the 1960s by the
30 State of New York to find out why new education **initiatives** had not succeeded, researchers at St John's University in New York City found that with each programme introduced into schools, some students

→

WORD BANK

surmised guessed

inventory detailed list

had benefited, obtaining better grades, while others remained the same and some students' grades declined.

35 The researchers were intrigued that the programmes helped some students while at the same time apparently disadvantaging other students. Perhaps, it was **surmised**, we all learn in different ways, and so we each have a unique learning style which responds well to some environments, and not to others. So for those students whose

40 learning style requires silence, bright lights, a hard chair and desk, the traditional school is the perfect learning environment. On the other hand, for those who learn best in exactly the opposite way, the global students, school frequently offers only discomfort, misunderstanding and even failure because it has not accommodated to their preferences.

45 Students with IQs over 145 are thought to be almost all global learners, and for some of them school can be a source of boredom and misery.

If teachers can adapt their classroom to accommodate students' learning styles, their students can flourish. It is easiest to do in a

50 primary classroom where children can choose whether to sit at their desks or sit in areas of the classroom kitted out with carpet, bean bags and armchairs. Children who like to listen to music while they learn can be equipped with personal stereos.

It is easy to identify individual student learning styles by means of a

55 104-question learning style **inventory** devised by academics at St John's University in New York City. When analysed by a company licensed by St. John's, a unique learning profile of each student is produced, telling exactly how that student's learning may be brought to its full potential. Analyses can be done on children from nursery age upwards – different

60 inventories are available for the differing age groups.

When any student is given this information, and told how to accommodate to it, then be ready for such comments as: "I conducted an experiment where I read all my Spanish notes into my tape player and went for a 40-minute run while listening to the tape. Reinforcing

65 new material kinesthetically turned out to be such a positive act that on the next test my usual grade of 70 per cent went up to 88 per cent." This was written by one of my students describing how a learning-style technique helped her learn new and difficult material.

One elementary school in North Carolina, having implemented

70 this programme, found its state-mandated test results reaching such highs that the state actually sent in officials to ensure that the school was not cheating!

WORD BANK

spouses a people's husband or wife

siblings brothers or sisters

mantra a word or phrase that is constantly repeated to help people meditate

Spouses tend to have opposite learning styles, as do siblings. **Siblings** of similar intelligence will sometimes have wildly different

75 school careers, one successful and the other struggling.

For these students, it might be that one learning style was accommodated, and the other not. With the need for improved education now at critical levels, this low-cost approach should be at least investigated. The brain is the organ of learning, just as the

80 heart is the organ of pumping. Thus the brain will learn, one way or another, because that's its nature.

Now, with the findings of this research, whether the brain learns in the classroom or on the street is up to the school and its response to this little **mantra**: "Teacher, if I don't learn the way you teach, why

85 don't you teach the way I learn?"

Basic reading skills

1 The writer of this article compares the classroom in the school William Shakespeare attended 400 years ago with a modern-day classroom.

   a List three things that the writer says are similar.

   b List three things that the writer says are different.

2 What are the three main types of learner the writer identifies in the article?

3 Look at the following learning techniques and decide whether they are most appropriate for an auditory, visual, tactile or kinesthetic learner.

Reading a textbook   **Conducting an experiment**   **Going to a museum**   **Listening to a lecture**

4 According to the writer, what type of school finds it easiest to adapt their classroom to accommodate students' different learning styles? Explain why this is.

5 Using your own words, explain what happened when a school in South Carolina identified the individual learning styles of its students.

6 Look again at the final paragraph.

   a Quote the mantra that the writer includes here.

   b Why do you think the writer refers to this as a mantra? Explain your ideas.

Advanced reading skills

1 The lead paragraph of a newspaper article should give the reader information on what the article is about.

   a Look again at the lead paragraph. Using your own words, summarize what the article is about.

   b Do you think this is an effective opening paragraph? Give reasons for your answer.

Key term

authoritative having authority and power

2a Pick out evidence from the text that supports the view that students learn in different ways.

2b How does the writer make this evidence sound **authoritative**? You could comment on the following phrases:

- 'based on more than 30 years of research'

- '104-question learning style inventory'

- 'devised by academics'

3a Find three quotations which suggest the negative effects of failing to accommodate different learning styles.

3b Choose one of your selected quotations and explain how it uses language to suggest these negative effects.

4 This article was included in the education section of *The Independent* newspaper. What changes would you make to the article to make it more interesting to a general readership?

Extended reading

Look back at the three texts you have read in this section. In your view, which text presents its ideas most effectively? Use some of these questions to structure your response:

- What is the text type and how does this affect the way ideas are presented?

- What key ideas are presented?

- How does the writer use language and structure to present these ideas?

- Does the writer have a specific viewpoint? Does the writer present other people's viewpoints?

- Did the text influence your point of view? Why or why not?

Extended writing

Write a guide for students about how to avoid distractions in the classroom. Draw on what you have learned from the texts you have read in this section. In your writing you could:

- explain why it is important to avoid distractions in the classroom

- give advice to students with different learning styles on how to avoid distractions

- use language and structure to help present information and ideas in the most effective way.

Remember to check the spelling, punctuation and grammar of your writing.

Early bird

Invent a gadget that could prevent students getting distracted in class. You could make this as weird or wonderful as you like! Write about your invention or draw a diagram with labels.

Source texts table

Text	Genre	Date
3.1 'Roald Dahl and me' by David Walliams	Newspaper article	2009
3.2 'A passion for books' by Sue Townsend	Essay	1992
3.3 'Juvenilia' by Sir Arthur Conan Doyle	Magazine article	1893

Big picture

Humans love stories. We read books, go to the cinema and watch stories on our TV screens. What are your earliest memories of being read to or reading? As we grow older, some of the stories we encountered in our youngest days stay in our minds. The characters we have met seem like friends, and their experiences help us with our own experiences, whether good or bad.

This section explores the stories that shape us and how they inspire different writers. You will read a newspaper article written by David Walliams on the influence of Roald Dahl, an extract from an essay by the 20th-century author Sue Townsend explaining the development of her passion for books in her childhood, and an extract from a magazine article written by the creator of Sherlock Holmes, Sir Arthur Conan Doyle, in which he describes his early experiences as a reader and a storyteller.

Skills

Key term

adjective a word that describes a noun

- Understand the meaning of a text
- Make inferences and refer to evidence in a text
- Comment on a writer's use of language and structure (including **adjectives**, viewpoints, factual information and paragraphing)
- Compare texts
- Practise writing an essay, drawing on techniques and ideas explored in your reading

Before reading

1 Draw a timeline from birth to the age you are now. Mark on this the different stages of your education so far, like in the example below.

birth   pre-school   infant school   junior school   secondary school

Note down on the timeline some of the different texts you remember from different stages of your life. Think about fiction texts (for example, novels, comic books) and non-fiction texts (magazines, websites).

2 Share your memories and timeline with a friend or partner. How are your reading experiences similar or different?

3 How has your reading changed over the years? Use the prompts below to write a reflective paragraph about the patterns in your reading habits:

- When and where do you like to read?

- What **genres** of texts do you like to read?

- How have your reading habits changed over the years?

You might want to use some of the sentence starters below:

- The first change I have noticed in my reading patterns is that…

- My earliest memories of reading include…

- A difference in the way I read now is…

- The kinds of text I enjoy have developed…

3.1 'Roald Dahl and me' by David Walliams, 2009

One of the most famous and successful children's writers of all time is Roald Dahl. In this article the actor, comedian and children's author David Walliams pays tribute to the work of Roald Dahl and describes how his own writing has been influenced by Dahl's fiction. Before you begin reading, note down what you already know about Roald Dahl and David Walliams. This might include details about the books they have written – titles, characters, plots – or facts about their lives.

Source text 3.1

WORD BANK

gauge judge

Before I started writing my first children's novel, *The Boy in the Dress*, I made a big mistake. I decided to re-read some of the books I had loved as a child. I wanted to try to **gauge** the right tone for a book for children, after years of co-writing an adult comedy show.
5 I devoured *Stig of the Dump*, *Peter Pan*, *Alice in Wonderland*, *The Lion, the Witch and the Wardrobe* and – my absolute favourite – *Charlie and the Chocolate Factory*. This last one instantly made me want to give up writing. It was perfect.

WORD BANK

enduringly long-lastingly

subtlety hidden details

conventional morality traditional ways of behaving

compelling fascinating

unfeasibly unexpectedly

eccentric unpredictable

cantankerous bad-tempered

I started reading more and more of Dahl's stories. *The Twits,*
Danny the Champion of the World, The BFG, George's Marvellous
Medicine, The Witches and *Fantastic Mr Fox*. Soon I realised that
they were all perfect in their own way. What really surprised me
was how different each was from the others; there was no apparent
formula. For example, the events depicted in *Danny the Champion*
of the World could happen in the real world, whereas those in *The*
BFG couldn't. So why is Roald Dahl, 20 years after his death and
40 years after he wrote some of his best-known works, one of the
most **enduringly** popular children's authors?

First, I think it's because he understood that children respond
to stories where they are empowered. Harry Potter may be the
most extreme example of this, but Dahl always empowers his child
characters with masterful **subtlety**. He never gives them magical
powers or makes them secret agents. Charlie lives in poverty but
finds a golden ticket; George happens upon a recipe that makes his
loathsome grandma change size; Danny has to drive his father's
car through the night. Dahl empowers them enough, but never too
much. It is interesting that he leaves George unable to remember
his magical recipe. [...]

Dahl is the master of cruelty. Witness what happens to all those
rotten children in Willy Wonka's factory. Augustus Gloop falls into
the chocolate river and is sucked through a giant pipe, Veruca Salt is
attacked by squirrels and disposed of down a rubbish chute, Violet
Beauregarde (what genius character names!) is turned into a giant
blueberry and Mike Teavee is shrunk. Reading it as a child, I was pretty
sure they had been killed, and looking at it again I got the feeling that
may have been what Dahl wanted. The children are glimpsed again
later in the story, but it feels like an afterthought to appease concerned
parents. In his story, George effectively kills his grandmother. She
is certainly dead at the end of the book. This lack of **conventional**
morality is extremely **compelling** for young readers, who feel as
though they are entering a thrillingly dangerous world.

When I was growing up in the 1970s and 1980s, Roald Dahl
was a regular on television. [...] In a way, though, he was not a great
ambassador for his work. As a child I was quite scared of him. Dahl
was **unfeasibly** tall (6ft 6in), bald, and dressed like an old professor.

He came across as an **eccentric** and **cantankerous** uncle, and didn't seem to have much warmth for the children who would telephone the shows with their questions. He was an outsider who sat alone in his shed all day, dreaming up more and more wicked
50 stories. Stories that you were absolutely desperate to read.

His narratives are surprisingly **anarchic** too. The stories of his I hadn't read as a child surprised me as an adult. There is nothing prescriptive or predictable about them, with little sense of narrative rules. Nothing reassuring. So many children's stories
55 want to have everything in their rightful place. Not Dahl's. Indeed, *The BFG* reads like a dream narrative, with the Queen making an appearance halfway through to save the day. In *The Twits*, a blacker-than-black comedy about an old couple who loathe each other, talking monkeys show up. Tim Burton changed the ending
60 of *Charlie* for his film version, adding a scene where Willy Wonka experiences family life for the first time with Charlie, his parents and grandparents. Burton forced a kind of **redemption** on Willy Wonka, but Dahl doesn't feel the need for a happy ending. Instead the book ends with Wonka whisking Charlie and his grandpa off in
65 his great glass elevator. [...]

Children are the toughest audience. If they find something boring they say so. If they don't like a book they will simply stop reading it. At school you might be forced to read **Shakespeare or Milton or Dickens**. Twenty years after his death, the beauty of
70 Dahl's status as an author is that his work is regarded as **populist** entertainment, which places him just outside the "great literature" bracket. Future generations of children will carry on reading his books simply because they want to, not because they have to, for the pure pleasure of **luxuriating** in Dahl's imagination. What
75 more could any writer ask for?

Basic reading skills

1   Create a list of five factual statements based on information from the text. The first one has been done for you.

   Before he wrote his first novel, Walliams re-read some children's books.

2   Look at the last two sentences in the first paragraph. David Walliams writes: 'This last one instantly made me want to give up writing. It was perfect.' Explain in your own words what he is implying.

3   Look again at the second paragraph. Identify the two Roald Dahl books that David Walliams contrasts and explain the key difference between these books.

4   David Walliams writes that 'Dahl is the master of cruelty'. List three examples that Walliams gives of how Dahl is cruel in his fiction.

5   Look at the fifth paragraph. David Walliams describes seeing Roald Dahl on television.

   a   Explain what he means when he says, 'he was not a great ambassador for his work'.

   b   Choose two words of your own to describe his impression of the writer.

6   In the final paragraph of his article, David Walliams writes that readers enjoy the 'pure pleasure of luxuriating in Dahl's imagination'. In your own words, describe what he means.

Advanced reading skills

1   It is clear that David Walliams admires Roald Dahl's work.

   a   Write down three features that he especially likes.

   b   If you had to give one overall reason for David Walliams' admiration, which would it be? How can you tell?

2   Look at the opening sentence of the article. David Walliams writes: 'Before I started writing my first children's novel, I made a big mistake'.

   Instead of the adjective 'big', he could have chosen major, large, significant or enormous.

   However, he chooses to use a short, simple word.

   a   If you were choosing a word instead of 'big', which of those four would you use? Explain why.

   b   Explain why you think David Walliams chose to use the short, simple word 'big'.

3   In the third paragraph, David Walliams writes about Roald Dahl's characters, especially the children at the heart of his books. He writes: 'He never gives them magical powers or makes them secret agents.'

He presents this as a positive feature of Roald Dahl's stories. Explain what you think he means and why you agree or disagree with his opinion.

4   Look at these other features that David Walliams identifies in Roald Dahl's writing:

- 'Lack of conventional morality'

- 'Master of cruelty'

- 'Anarchic'

Explain how David Walliams gives you the impression that these are positive features.

5   Which point in the article do you most agree with or disagree with? Write a few sentences to explain your viewpoint. Quote David Walliams' words if it helps you to support your case.

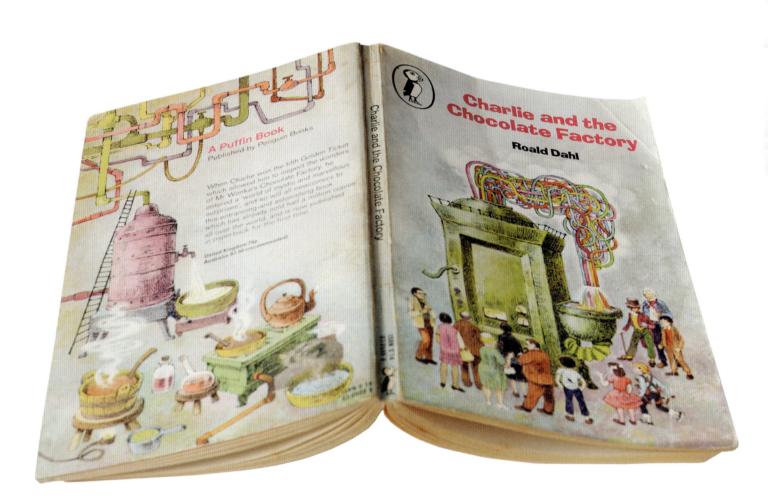

3.2 'A passion for books' by Sue Townsend, 1992

Sue Townsend was a hugely successful author and playwright, best known for her creation of a comical teenage character called Adrian Mole. In this essay, she explains when she started reading and how it grew into an obsession. As you read, decide what you think was the biggest turning point for Townsend in the development of her love of books.

Source text 3.2

WORD BANK

dyspeptic irritable

rummage sale sale of second-hand items

***William* books** short, humorous stories about a schoolboy who was always getting into trouble and having adventures

Red Arrows an acrobatic flight display team who often perform at national celebrations

Woolworth's a popular high-street store in the 20th century

Sotherby's a famous art dealer

I was eight before I could read. My teacher was a nasty drunken woman who looked like a **dyspeptic** badger. I'm forty-six now and she is long dead, but my heart almost stops if I see anyone resembling her stomping along the pavement towards me.

5   I learnt to read during the three weeks I was away from school with a spectacular case of mumps. (Mumps *were* mumps in the 1950s.) My mother went to a **rummage sale** and came back with a pile of ***William* books** written by Richmal Crompton, a person I assumed to be a man. I looked at the illustrations and laughed,

10 then I tried to read the captions underneath these delightful scratchy drawings. My mother helped me out and slowly and mysteriously the black squiggles turned into words which turned into sentences, which turned into stories. I could read.

    There should have been a hundred-gun salute. The **Red Arrows**

15 should have flown overhead. The night sky should have blazed with fireworks.

    I joined the library thirsting after more *William* books. I read one a day and then two a day, then I ran out and fumbled along the library bookshelves pulling out books at random. Nothing was ever

20 as good as *William*, but the die was cast, I was addicted to print.

    Christmas came, and with it a stack of books in the **Woolworth's** classics series. They had serious red covers, and gilt lettering: *Treasure Island* and *Kidnapped*, R. D. Blackmore's *Lorna Doone, Heidi, Little Women,* Harriet Beecher Stowe's *Uncle Tom's*

25 *Cabin.* In the front of each book there was a coloured illustration, and when I had read the last page I would turn back to the beginning and study this picture as closely as a **Sotherby's** expert; trying to extract more meaning and more pleasure. I've always felt a great sadness on finishing a book I've enjoyed. And a strong

30 reluctance to actually close the book and put it on a shelf.[...]

    During the junior school holidays I would often read three books a day. The local librarian used to interrogate me on the contents, convinced that I was showing off, though there was nobody to

←

WORD BANK

counterpane a bedspread

Jane Eyre a classic novel by Charlotte Brontë about the life of a Victorian governess

gabardine a tough woven fabric traditionally used to make coats

impress in my immediate circle. Most adults took my passion for
35 books as a sign of derangement. 'Your brain will burst,' was a
common warning, one that I took seriously. When reading I half
expected my head to explode and hit the ceiling. It didn't put me off.
Reading became the most important thing in my life. My favourite
place to read was on my bed, lying on a pink cotton **counterpane**,
40 and if I had a bag of sweets next to me, I was in heaven.

The first book I lost a night's sleep over was ***Jane Eyre***. It was
winter and our house wasn't heated – apart from a coal fire in the
living room. I read in bed. My fingers and arms froze, my nails went
blue. Frost formed on the inside of the window panes, but I could not
45 put *Jane Eyre* down. I loved Jane. Snow fell, a few birds began to sing,
my eyes drooped but I had to read on. Who had started the fire? Who
was the mad creature in the attic? I ate my porridge reading. I walked
to school reading. I read in each lesson until the morning milk break.
I finished the last page in the school cloakroom, surrounded by wet
50 **gabardine** mackintoshes. I felt very lonely. I wanted to talk about
Jane Eyre. There were so many references I didn't understand, but I
made no attempt to talk about that or any other book.

Reading became a secret obsession; I would drop a book guiltily
if anyone came into a room. I went nowhere without a book – the
55 lavatory, a bus journey, walking to school.

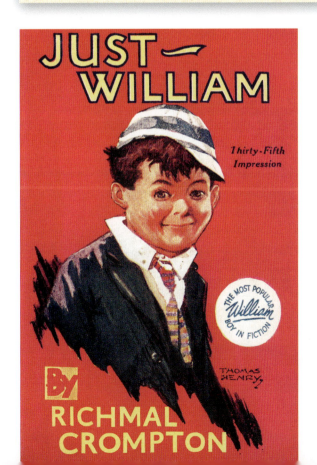

Basic reading skills

Key words

facts things that are known to have happened or be true

opinions what someone thinks or believes

1   Re-read the first paragraph.

   a List three **facts** the writer gives in this paragraph.

   b List two **opinions** the writer gives in this paragraph.

2   Now look at the second paragraph. Using your own words, summarize how the writer learned to read.

3   'There should have been a hundred-gun salute. The Red Arrows should have flown overhead. The night sky should have blazed with fireworks.' What impression does this quotation give you of the writer's emotions when she learned to read?

4   Pick out three quotations that suggest the writer was a keen reader when she was young.

5   What suggests the librarian didn't believe the writer had read all the books that she borrowed from the library?

6   How does the writer suggest that reading was a 'secret obsession'? Using information from the text, explain why you think the writer had to keep her reading a secret.

Key words

simile a comparison where one thing is compared to another using the words *like* or *as*

1   Look at the first paragraph and identify the **simile** the writer uses to describe her teacher. Explain the effect this creates.

2   Pick out all the different places the writer says she used to read.

   a What impression does this give you of the writer?

   b Explain the effect this use of repetition creates.

3   The writer says: 'When reading I half expected my head to explode and hit the ceiling. It didn't put me off.'

   a Explain how the writer uses humour in this quotation.

   b Pick out another quotation that you think creates humour and explain your choice.

4   Which book do you think was the most important to the writer in her childhood? Refer to evidence from the text to support your choice.

5   'Reading became the most important thing in my life.' Explain how the writer uses language to suggest how important reading was to her.

6   Look at the following student's statement about the text:

I think books were the writer's friend.

Argue for or against this statement, drawing on evidence from the text.

3.3 'Juvenilia' by Sir Arthur Conan Doyle, 1893

Sir Arthur Conan Doyle was born in Edinburgh on 22 May 1859. As a child he was an avid reader, particularly enjoying the adventure novels of R. M. Ballantyne and Captain Mayne Reid. From the age of 11 he attended Stonyhurst College, a boarding school in Lancashire, where he began to develop his talents as a storyteller. In the following extract from a magazine article first published in *The Idler* magazine in January 1893, Conan Doyle describes his early years as a reader and writer.

Source text 3.3

WORD BANK

Romanticists followers of the **Romantic** style in art and literature

Romantic an artistic and literary movement in the late 18th and early 19th centuries, it valued imagination and emotion our rationality

aphorism a short witty saying

daguerreotype an early type of photograph

I was six at the time, and have a very distinct recollection of the achievement [of becoming a writer]. It was written, I remember, upon foolscap paper, in what might be called a fine
5   bold hand – four words to the line, and was illustrated by marginal pen-and-ink sketches by the author. There was a man in it, and there was a tiger. I forget which was the hero, but it didn't matter much, for they became
10 blended into one about the time when the tiger met the man. I was a realist in the age of the **Romanticists**, I described at some length, both verbally and pictorially the untimely end of that wayfarer. But when the tiger had absorbed him, I found myself slightly embarrassed as to how my story was to go
15 on. 'It is very easy to get people into scrapes, and very hard to get them out again,' I remarked, and I have often had cause to repeat the precocious **aphorism** of my childhood. On this occasion the situation was beyond me, and my book, like my man, was engulfed in my tiger. There is an old family bureau with secret drawers, in
20 which lie little locks of hair tied up in circles, and black silhouettes and dim **daguerreotypes**, and letters which seem to have been written in the lightest of straw coloured inks. Somewhere there lies my primitive manuscript, where my tiger, like a many-hooped barrel with a tail to it, still envelops the hapless stranger whom he has
25 taken in.

Then came my second book, which was told and not written, but which was a much more ambitious effort than the first. Between the two, four years had elapsed, which were mainly spent in reading. It is rumoured that a special meeting of a library committee was held in
30 my honour, at which a bye-law was passed that no subscriber should be permitted to change his book more than three times a day. Yet, even with these limitations, by the aid of a well-stocked bookcase at home,

I managed to enter my tenth year with a good deal in my head that I could never have learned in the class-rooms.

35 I do not think that life has any joy to offer so complete, so soul-filling as that which comes upon the imaginative lad, whose spare time is limited, but who is able to snuggle down into a corner with his book knowing that the next hour is all his own. And how vivid and fresh it all is! Your very heart and soul are out on the prairies and
40 the oceans with your hero. It is you who act and suffer and enjoy… You lie out upon the topsail yard, and get jerked by the flap of the sail into the Pacific, where you cling on to the leg of an albatross, and so keep afloat until the comic **boatswain** turns up with his crew of volunteers to handspike you into safety. What a magic it is,
45 this stirring of the boyish heart and mind! Long **ere** I came to my teens I had traversed every sea and knew the Rockies like my own back garden. How often had I sprung upon the back of the charging buffalo and so escaped him! It was an everyday emergency to have to set the prairie on fire in front of me in order to escape from the fire
50 behind, or to run a mile down a brook to throw the bloodhounds off my trail. I had **creased** horses, I had shot down rapids, I had strapped on my mocassins **hindforemost** to conceal my tracks, I had lain under water with a reed in my mouth, and I had feigned madness to escape the torture… It was all more real than the reality.
55 Since those days I have in very truth both shot bears and harpooned whales, but the performance was flat compared with the first time that I did it with Mr. Ballantyne or Captain Mayne Reid at my elbow.

In the fullness of time I was packed off to a public school, and in some way it was discovered by my playmates that I had more than
60 my share of the **lore** after which they hankered. There was my debut as a story-teller. On a wet half-holiday I have been elevated on to a desk, and with an audience of little boys all squatting on the floor, with their chins upon their hands, I have talked myself husky over the misfortunes of my heroes. Week in and week out those unhappy
65 men have battled and striven and groaned for the amusement of that little circle. I was bribed with pastry to continue these efforts, and I remember that I always stipulated for tarts down and strict business, which shows that I was born to be a member of the Authors' Society. Sometimes, too, I would stop dead in the very thrill of a crisis, and
70 could only be set agoing again by apples. When I had got as far as 'Slowly, slowly, the door turned upon its hinges, and with eyes which were dilated with horror, the wicked Marquis saw…' I knew that I had my audience in my power. And thus my second book was evolved.

WORD BANK

boatswain a ship's officer in charge of rigging, boats and anchors

ere before

creased captured

hindforemost back to front

lore a set of facts about a particular topic or culture

Basic reading skills

1   Look again at the first paragraph. Using your own words, briefly summarize what happened in the first story Sir Arthur Conan Doyle wrote.

2   Where does he say his first story is now?

3   Look at the second paragraph beginning, 'Then came my second book…'. Pick out the quotation that you think best suggests that the writer was a keen reader as a child.

4   List five exciting situations that the writer claims to have experienced through his reading.

5   What payment does he receive from his classmates for his storytelling at public school?

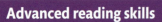

Advanced reading skills

1   Re-read the opening paragraph. What impression do you get of Sir Arthur Conan Doyle as a six-year-old? In your answer you should comment on:

   ■ what he remembers about his first story

   ■ his feelings about this

   ■ what these suggest about his personality.

2   Look again at the paragraph beginning, 'I do not think that life has any joy…'. How does the language used help to create a sense of the excitement the writer found in the stories he read? You should comment on:

   ■ the use of the **first** and **second person**, for example, 'I remarked…', 'You lie…'

   ■ the verbs chosen to describe the action he found in his childhood reading

   ■ his choice of vocabulary and descriptive details

   ■ his choice of **sentence forms**.

Key terms

first person the writer uses 'I' and 'we'

second person addressing the reader as 'you'

sentence forms sentence types (that is, statement, question, command, exclamation) and sentence structures (that is, simple, minor, multi-clause)

3 Read the following quotation from the extract: 'It was all more real than the reality.'

Explain whether you think this extract supports or contradicts this statement about the power of stories. Give reasons for your answer, referring to the text of the extract.

4 The writer describes his real experience of shooting bears and harpooning whales as 'flat'. How might we describe these activities nowadays, and why?

5 How does the writer create a sense of his growing power as a storyteller? Think about how both language and structure are used to build a picture of him as an author and convey his abilities as a storyteller.

Extended reading

Revisit the article about Roald Dahl by David Walliams and the article by Sir Arthur Conan Doyle in order to answer the following question.

Compare the views the two writers present about the influence that books have on children. In your answer, you could:

- compare the views and experiences they present, identifying any similarities and differences between these
- compare the methods the writers use to convey their ideas
- explore your own thoughts and responses to these as a reader
- support your ideas with references to both texts.

Extended writing

Choose a writer whose books you know well. It might be someone you read when you were younger, or an author whose works you currently enjoy. Like David Walliams, write an essay or article describing what you admire about the writer's books. You could include:

- biographical information about the writer's background
- factual information about the books – how many the author has written, their titles and themes
- a description of your first encounter with this writer's work and how you responded
- an appreciation of the writer's style (how he or she writes, how the plots work, memorable characters)
- advice to the reader on which book to read first and why.

Remember to check the spelling, punctuation and grammar of your writing.

Early bird

From Augustus Gloop to Violet Beauregarde, author Roald Dahl had a talent for inventing memorable character names. Think up some new ones for teachers, mysterious creatures, heroes or villains. Be as creative as you can.

Modern living

Source texts table

Texts	Genre	Date
4.1 'Hotel unveils ROBOT butler' by Josh Gardner	Newspaper article	2014
4.2 'The servantless house' (author unknown)	Newspaper article	1921
4.3 'Duties of the Lady's Maid' from *Mrs Beeton's Book of Household Management* by Isabella Beeton	Guide	1861

Big picture

For hundreds of years people have been looking for ways to make our lives more comfortable. From hiring servants in the 19th century to the invention of labour-saving devices in the 20th century and high-tech gadgets in the 21st, 'modern living' has seen some major changes through the ages. What comforts in your own home do you enjoy that your ancestors would not have had?

In this section you will read three non-fiction texts that explore aspects of modern living in the time they were written: a newspaper article from the 21st century about a robot butler, a newspaper article from the early 20th century comparing the costs of employing servants with buying labour-saving devices such as the vacuum cleaner, and an extract from *Mrs Beeton's Book of Household Management*, first published in 1861, which provides advice on the duties of a lady's maid in a Victorian home.

Skills

- Understand the meaning of a text
- Make inferences and refer to evidence in a text
- Comment on a writer's use of language and structure
- Explore the techniques used by a writer to communicate views and ideas
- Compare texts
- Practise writing a newspaper article, drawing on techniques and ideas explored in your reading

Before reading

1 Think about your own home. What do you like most about it? Which are your favourite rooms or features? What would you change about it?

2 Create a timetable for a typical Saturday that you spend at home. List the devices you or your family use and why, for example, a laptop to shop online.

3 Think of two advantages and one disadvantage of employing a servant such as a butler or maid in your home.

4.1 'Hotel unveils ROBOT butler' by Josh Gardner, 2014

The following newspaper article explains how one hotel in America is using a robot butler. As you read the text, think about the advantages and disadvantages of having a robot butler rather than a human butler.

Source text 4.1

WORD BANK

bellhop hotel porter who helps guests with luggage and room service

R2D2 a robot in the Star Wars films

Wall-E a robot in the science-fiction comedy film of the same name

The Jetsons an American sitcom about a futuristic family

CEO Chief Executive Officer, the senior leader in an organization or company

Hotel unveils ROBOT butler that makes automated room service calls and accepts reviews from guests instead of tips

A California hotel introduced a new **bellhop** on Tuesday: meet A.L.O., the industry's first robot butler.

Shortened to Botlr, the high tech hospitality technology will ferry amenities from the front desk of the Aloft in Cupertino to any
5   of its 150 rooms in just three minutes or less.

The Starwood company is using its Silicon Valley location as a test bed for the speedy **R2D2**-like drone.

'As soon as A.L.O. entered the room, we knew it was what we were looking for. A.L.O. has the work ethic of **Wall-E**, the humor of
10 Rosie from **The Jetsons** and reminds me of my favorite childhood robot, R2D2.' Brian McGuinness of Starwood's Speciality Select Brands said in a press release Tuesday.

The 3-foot tall robot, made by the firm Savioke, features a smart vinyl collar and even a name tag.
15 While running everything from razors to mail to Aloft guests, A.L.O. moves at a fast clip of up to 4mph.

Meanwhile Savioke says it manuevers through elevators and communicates easily with guests and staff.

'All of us at Savioke have seen the look of delight on those guests
20 who receive a room delivery from a robot,' said Steve Cousins, **CEO** of Savioke.

Starwood and Savioke hope to use the robot as a way to funnel existing human staff towards more sensitive tasks rather than a death knell for bellhops.
25 With the delivery complete, the robot then asks for a review. If the guest inputs a positive remark on the built-in screen, the robot does a happy dance.

The accomplished drone then zips back to the elevator, sends a message instead of hitting the down button and returns to the
30 lobby where it plugs itself in and awaits a new task.

→

So how exactly will guests experience A.L.O.?

According to the *New York Times*, the robot will arrive to guests' doors soon after they put in a request and will automatically place a call to the room instead of knocking.

35   When the robot's sensors indicate the door has opened, it lifts its storage bin lid to reveal the requested item.

Basic reading skills

1a   What is the name of the robot butler, mentioned in the first paragraph?

1b   Explain why you think this is an appropriate name.

2a   In the second paragraph, what is the term 'robot butler' shortened to?

2b   Again, explain why you think this is an appropriate name.

3a   Identify three fictional robots that the robot butler is compared to.

3b   Choose one of these fictional robots and explain why this comparison is appropriate.

4   How does the robot butler respond if it receives a positive review? Pick the correct statement from the list below.

- It lifts its storage bin lid.
- It does a happy dance.
- It looks delighted.
- It plugs itself in and awaits a new task.

Key term

direct speech when the words a person has spoken are relayed to the reader exactly, using speech marks

5   The article says: 'Starwood and Savioke hope to use the robot as a way to funnel existing human staff towards more sensitive tasks rather than a death knell for bellhops'. Using your own words, explain what the term 'death knell' means here.

Advanced reading skills

1   Explain how this article gives you the impression that the robot butler is a worthwhile invention.

2   The writer uses lots of short, single-sentence paragraphs. Pick out some examples and explain why you think the writer has chosen to structure the article in this way.

3   The article includes **direct speech** from Brian McGuinness and Steve Cousins. Why do you think the writer has chosen to do this? Explain the effect created by the use of direct speech from each person quoted in the text.

4   Do you think this article would have appeared in the technology section or the travel section of *The Daily Mail*? Refer to evidence from the text to support your answer.

4.2 'The servantless house', 1921

The following newspaper article was first published in *The Guardian* newspaper on 28 December 1921. At this time, labour-saving devices to help with housework such as the electric vacuum cleaner were becoming more readily available. In this article, the writer compares the cost of purchasing such devices with the cost of employing a servant to carry out these jobs for you. As you read, think about the different clues the article gives you about the time it was written.

Source text 4.2

WORD BANK

procured obtained or acquired

housewifery the jobs carried out by a married woman around the home

wear and tear wear or damage from continuous use

28 December 1921: Mechanical appliances and other labour savers can be **procured** to lighten considerably the tasks of **housewifery**

The general idea that labour-saving machinery is too expensive to be installed in ordinary houses calls for an investigation of the cost of running a house with and without a servant.

There are, broadly speaking, two classes of people without servants to-day – those who cannot afford to keep one on account of the present high wages and cost of living, and those who, while not well off in the common sense of the term, have enough money to keep at least one maid but who prefer not to do so. Whatever the cause, the servantless housewife is faced with the same problem of getting the work done as best she can.

In pre-war days the housekeeper, while perfectly aware of the time and labour involved in polishing brass, cleaning stair-rods, sweeping carpets, and other frequent tasks of housework, did not bother herself very much about these things so long as there were servants to do the work: but now with servants unaffordable, unobtainable, or considered undesirable a keen application has led to the provision and development of all sorts of labour-saving appliances. Moreover, it is obviously these labour-saving devices, in conjunction with well-planned work, that can make it possible to run a house successfully and conveniently without a maid.

Relative Costs

A comparison of the relative cost of a maid and of labour-saving machinery will prove that the latter is not such an extravagance as might appear at a first glance. It may be taken as a general rule that a good general servant cannot be obtained to-day for less than £35 to £45 a year, and at present prices it will probably cost £1 a week for her keep. To this must be added, if an accurate comparison is to be made, the cost in **wear and tear**, in breakages, and in lack

WORD BANK

conscientious careful and honest about doing your work properly

annual expenditure the amount of money spent every year

outlay the amount of money spent on something

service wagon a hostess trolley in which cooked food could be kept hot and served

anthracite a kind of hard coal

exorbitant too expensive

of economy of fuel and light. The house not being hers it is only human that a maid, unless exceptionally **conscientious**, will not be always on the watch to prevent unnecessary use of gas, water, &c., and to economise in every possible way.

35 Considering all these points the cost of having a maid may be summed up as follows:—

Wages – £40

Keep per year – £52

Breakages – £3

40 *Wear and tear, &c. – £3*

Total – £98

This, it must be remembered, is an **annual expenditure**. An **outlay** of the most essential labour-saving devices can be estimated as follows:—

45 *An electric vacuum cleaner – £16*

A fuelless cooker – £5

A service waggon *– £4*

Stainless knives – £5

Gas fires or electric radiators – £15

50 **Anthracite** *stove – £8*

Small electrical equipment – £7

Total – £60

Thus for an outlay of £60 enough mechanical appliances and other labour-savers can be procured to lighten considerably the

55 tasks of housewifery.

The fact that this is but an initial outlay expense must be emphasised, since a maid's cost is continuous. After a year or two there is but a small proportion of expenditure as compared with what was formerly the case with a servant, and the housewife will

60 find herself with a considerable balance in hand and will be able to add to her list of appliances, proving each to be a thoroughly good investment.

It is only when the cost of appliances is regarded without consideration or comparison that such equipment can be vetoed

65 as **exorbitant** and only accessible to millionaires. Mechanical labour is more certain, less tiring and altogether more reliable than human labour, and the wise housewife will welcome it as the means of solving her household difficulties and giving her freedom for other interests.

Basic reading skills

1 Look again at the paragraph beginning, 'The general idea…'.

   a What does the writer suggest this article is going to be about?

   b What reason does the writer give for writing this article?

2 Identify the two types of people who don't employ servants, according to the writer.

3 Look again at the paragraph beginning, 'In pre-war days…'.

   a List three tasks the writer suggests that servants carried out in this period.

   b List three reasons the writer gives why servants might not be able to carry out these tasks.

4 Look at the section entitled 'Relative costs'.

   a How much in total does the writer say a homeowner would spend on a maid in a year?

   b How much in total does the writer say a homeowner would spend buying essential labour-saving devices?

   c Re-read the paragraph beginning, 'The fact that this is…'. Explain another advantage of buying essential labour-saving devices that the writer gives here.

5 Does the writer recommend employing a maid or buying labour-saving devices?

Key terms

unbiased impartial, not favouring one side more than the other

rule of three (also called 'tricolon') linking three points or features for impact

Advanced reading skills

1 In this article, the writer compares the cost of purchasing such devices with the cost of employing a servant to carry out these jobs for you. Do you think the writer presents this comparison in an **unbiased** way? Refer to evidence from the text to support your answer.

2 The writer uses the **rule of three** to emphasize certain points. Look at this example: 'Mechanical labour is more certain, less tiring and altogether more reliable than human labour.'

   a How does this use of the rule of three support the writer's viewpoint?

   b Pick out another quotation from the article that uses the rule of three and explain the effect this creates.

3 How does the structure of the article help the reader to evaluate which is the best option: employing a maid or buying labour-saving devices? In your answer you should comment on:

   ■ the opening of the article and the ideas this introduces

   ■ what the focus of each paragraph is and how this helps the reader

   ■ the use of lists in the article and the effects these create

   ■ the ending of the article and how this links to the beginning.

4 This newspaper article was first published in 1921. Explain how the language and ideas in the article reflect the time in which it was written.

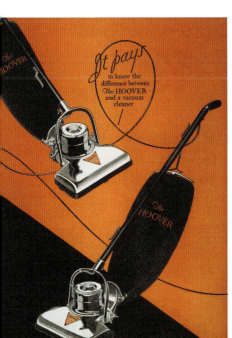

4.3 'Duties of the Lady's Maid' from *Mrs Beeton's Book of Household Management* by Isabella Beeton, 1861

The following text is an extract from *Mrs Beeton's Book of Household Management* by Isabella Beeton, first published in 1861. This bestselling guide provided readers with advice about running a home in Victorian Britain. In this extract the writer gives guidance about the duties that a lady's maid would be expected to carry out in a respectable household. As you read, think about the different tasks that are described and whether you find any of these unusual.

Source text 4.3

WORD BANK

strewed scattered over a surface

discretion freedom to decide things and take action according to your own judgement

countenance face or facial expression

[I]f the rooms are carpeted, she should sweep them carefully, having previously **strewed** the room with moist tea-leaves, dusting every table and chair, taking care to penetrate to every corner, and moving every article of furniture that is portable. This done satisfactorily,

5 and having cleaned the dressing-glass, polished up the furniture and the ornaments, and made the glass jug and basin clean and bright, emptied all slops, emptied the water-jugs and filled them with fresh water, and arranged the rooms, the dressing-room is ready for the mistress when she thinks proper to appear.

10 The dressing-room thoroughly in order, the same thing is to be done in the bedroom, in which she will probably be assisted by the housemaid to make the bed and empty the slops. In making the bed, she will study her lady's wishes, whether it is to be hard or soft, sloping or straight, and see that it is done accordingly.

15 Having swept the bedroom with equal care, dusted the tables and chairs, chimney-ornaments, and put away all articles of dress left from yesterday, and cleaned and put away any articles of jewellery, her next care is to see, before her mistress goes out, what requires replacing in her department, and furnish her with a list of them, that she may

20 use her **discretion** about ordering them. All this done, she may settle herself down to any work on which she is engaged, this will consist chiefly in mending; which is first to be seen to; everything, except stockings, being mended before washing. Plain work will probably be one of the lady's-maid's chief employments.

25 A waiting-maid, who wishes to make herself useful, will study the fashion-books with attention, so as to be able to aid her mistress's judgment in dressing, according to the prevailing fashion, with such modifications as her style of **countenance** requires. She will also, if she has her mistress's interest at heart, employ her spare time in

30 repairing and making up dresses which have served one purpose, to

WORD BANK

unfitted not suitable

render to cause a person or thing to become something

exigencies demands

serve another also; or turning many things, **unfitted** for her mistress to use, for the younger branches of the family. The lady's-maid may thus **render** herself invaluable to her mistress, and increase her own happiness in so doing. The **exigencies** of fashion and luxury are
35 such, that all ladies except those of the very highest rank, will consider themselves fortunate in having about them a thoughtful person, capable of diverting their finery to a useful purpose.

Basic reading skills

1 Re-read the first paragraph.

  a List three things which a lady's maid should do to get the dressing-room ready.

  b Pick out two quotations that suggest that a lady's maid should take great care when cleaning the room.

  c Look again at the phrase, 'the dressing-room is ready for the mistress when she thinks proper to appear'. Using your own words, explain what you think the writer means here.

2 Which room should the lady's maid prepare after getting the dressing-room ready?

3 What does the writer suggest will be one of the main tasks of a lady's maid? Pick out the quotation that suggests this.

4 Re-read the paragraph beginning, 'A waiting-maid, who wishes to make herself useful…'. Using your own words, summarize the key advice given here in a single sentence.

Advanced reading skills

1 What impression do you get of the duties of a lady's maid from this extract? Use a spider diagram to collect all the information you can about these from the text.

2 Which of the following characteristics do you think the extract suggests a lady's maid needs to have? For each one that you select, pick out a quotation from the extract that you think demonstrates the need for this characteristic. The first one has been done for you.

strong – 'moving every article of furniture that is portable'

diligent

dedicated

lazy

creative

thoughtful

Key term

tone a manner of expression in speech or writing

3 Read what this student says about the **tone** of this extract.

I think the writer creates quite a strict tone – it sounds as if she's ordering you about.

Do you agree or disagree with this statement? Justify your answer with reference to the text.

4 Write down three quotations from the text that show it was written in the 19th century. Think about:

- the information and ideas presented
- the writer's choice of vocabulary
- the sentence forms used.

Extended reading

Compare the two newspaper articles you have read in this section about the robot butler and about the servantless house. Which do you think presents its ideas in the most effective way? Use some or all of these questions to structure your response.

- What features of the newspaper article does each text use and what effects do these create?
- How do the writers hook their reader's interest and keep them reading?
- Does each writer's use of language and sentence forms help to convey the ideas they want to present?
- How does the way each article is structured contribute to its effectiveness?

Extended writing

Write a newspaper article about the benefits of employing a servant in the 21st-century home. In your article you can draw on information and ideas from the texts you have read in this section.

As you write, think about:

- the different features of a newspaper article
- how the opening of your article can hook the reader's attention
- how you can use language to suggest the benefits of employing a servant
- how you can structure your article to present information and ideas in the most effective way
- how you can link the ending of your article with the opening.

Remember to check the spelling, punctuation and grammar of your writing.

Early bird

Young people are less likely to read newspapers than older people. Do you think this is a good or bad thing? Try to think of as many arguments as you can to support your point of view.

Source texts table

Text	Genre	Date
5.1 'Top tips for creative writing' by Jacqueline Wilson	Blog	2016
5.2 Letter to Joan Lancaster by C. S. Lewis	Letter	1956
5.3 *The Life of Charlotte Brontë* by Elizabeth Gaskell	Biography	1857

Big picture

From short story competitions to online storytelling communities where teenagers post fan fiction, in some ways creative writing has never seemed more popular. What do you like about writing stories and what do you dislike?

For some people, the process of writing a story can seem difficult and rather mysterious. In this section you will read three non-fiction texts that reveal some secrets of the creative writing life: a blog post from the bestselling author Dame Jacqueline Wilson giving her tips about how to write a brilliant story; a letter from C. S. Lewis, the creator of *The Chronicles of Narnia*, giving advice to an aspiring writer; and an extract from *The Life of Charlotte Brontë* by Elizabeth Gaskell, a biography of the 19th-century author of *Jane Eyre*.

Skills

- Understand the meaning of a text

- Make inferences and refer to evidence in a text

- Comment on a writer's use of language and structure (including the effects of punctuation, italics, vocabulary choices and dialogue)

- Compare texts

- Practise writing a letter, drawing on techniques and ideas explored in your reading

Before reading

1   The writers of the non-fiction texts in this section are themselves all writers of fiction. Would this make you more or less likely to take notice of the information and advice they give about creative writing? Give reasons for your answer.

2   All writing is communication. Look at the following purposes for writing and match each of them up to the most appropriate form.

Purpose	Form
To entertain	Letter
To inform	Newspaper article
To describe	Autobiography
To provide advice	Novel
To persuade	Leaflet

Give reasons for your decisions.

5.1 'Top tips for creative writing' by Jacqueline Wilson, 2016

Jacqueline Wilson is one of the most successful writers of stories for children and young adults. In the following blog written for the website of the bookseller WH Smith, to tie in with their creative writing competition, she shares her secrets about writing successful stories.

Before you read the blog, try to predict the advice you think she might give. Think about your own reading and what ingredients you believe a captivating story needs. Then skim the blog to see how Jacqueline Wilson uses five headings to structure her top tips. From these headings refine your predictions about what her advice will be.

Source text 5.1

WORD BANK

foundling a child abandoned by his or her parents

1. How to Come Up With Ideas

It's the most frequently asked question: Where do you get your ideas from?

5   Sometimes it can be something you see by chance. I saw a heavily tattooed woman with two small daughters in Central Park, and my own daughter Emma whispered that they looked like the sort of family I'd write about. That's how I wrote *The Illustrated Mum*.

    Another gift was seeing photographs of children in my local
10 newspaper, all needing foster parents – this gave me the idea for *The Story of Tracy Beaker*.

    Just occasionally other people give me ideas – talk about the Director of the **Foundling** Museum asking if I'd ever consider writing a book about a foundling child – that's how *Hetty Feather*
15 sprang to life. Everyone gets their ideas in different ways.

2. How to Create Characters

I think the most important part of writing a story is getting to know your characters and making them seem real.

    Did you ever have imaginary friends when you were little? It's a
20 similar process. Hold conversations with your characters in your head. Don't just think about their looks, though I always like to give some idea what sort of hairstyle my girls have, and what sort of clothes they wear. But mostly I care what they're like inside. Are they happy, sad, shy, cheeky, funny, naughty? What are their
25 hobbies? What are their favourite television programmes? What's their favourite food? Do they like school? What's their best subject?

How do they get on with their mum or dad and siblings? Do they have a best friend? Do they want a best friend?

30   Think it all through, jot things down. You probably won't need to put half these things in your story but somehow it will help bring your characters alive on the page.

3. How to Start Your Story

This is the difficult bit! No-one likes looking at a blank page or screen. It's so hard to know how to start.

35   Everyone always says a story needs a really good eye-catching beginning – but of course that makes you go all self-conscious and unable to think of even one simple sentence.

    My tip would be to pretend you've got the most amazing piece of news and you're dashing into school to tell your best friend all
40 about it, and you just have to seize hold of them and give them the whole story straight away, making it as amusing and astonishing as possible so that you keep their full attention. I don't think you need several paragraphs of description and explanation before you get started on the story. Jump straight in. [...]

45 ### 4. How to Make Something Happen

Think of all the stories you've ever read, short stories, small books, huge great long books with hundreds of pages. They start. Then something happens. Often lots of things. And then they finish.

    It doesn't matter what sort of story you write, it's good to have
50 a bit of conflict – a bit of a struggle, something going wrong, something surprising – and your main character has to try to sort it all out.

    A princess might be locked up in a castle and she has to escape. A boy has lost his dog and has to find him. A dinosaur is suddenly
55 spotted walking down the High Street, nibbling the treetops. It's up to you to let the story evolve. Sometimes it's good to work it all out beforehand so you don't get stuck halfway through.

    Though sometimes it works just to write at white-hot speed and see what happens without planning anything at all. There's no
60 one way of writing. Everyone's different. If you've got started on your story but are stuck in the middle, try talking inside your head to your main character. Ask them what would really worry them? Then write it, and see how they cope.

5. How to End a Story

65 That's the best bit. You've written and written, and now you've nearly finished the story. You can't wait to write THE END after the last line.

It's a terrible temptation to hurry things along, because if you're anything like me you just want to be finished with the whole thing.

70 I used to find I wrote the last few pages of my stories too quickly, in a hasty scrappy sort of way, and then an editor (they're a bit like your teacher, and even more picky) would suggest I rewrite part and expand it and think it all through carefully.

Now I try to give the last chapter even more time and attention

75 than the first. I try to round everything off in a satisfying way. That doesn't mean I always spell everything out. Sometimes I deliberately leave my readers to work out what's going to happen next, though I always give a heavy hint. (Lots of you want to know if Lily gets reunited with her family in *Lily Alone* – or does Destiny

80 make it as a famous singer in *Little Darlings* – or will Hetty ever get together with Jem?) I wanted to keep all the options open – but if you find my endings disconcerting you're always free to write your own versions.[...]

So, let's say you've taken your time over your ending and are

85 pleased with your story. I'm afraid you've still got a little work to do, especially if it's a story for school, for a special project, for a competition. Read it through. See if there are parts that don't seem very important, or they're maybe simply a bit boring. How can you improve them? Could you pop something new in that

90 will make your story seem more interesting? Have you checked all your spellings and remembered all your punctuation? I know, these are the boring parts. I hate fussing over everything too – but it's truly worth it. It's often only when I've got to this stage that a sudden really good idea occurs to me. I don't like rewriting – but it's

95 generally vitally necessary.

You want your story to be as good as possible, don't you?

I hope you all feel inspired now.

Have a go!

Basic reading skills

1 In her first tip, Jacqueline Wilson gives three ways that she gets ideas. Which of these is not one that she mentions?

> **A.** Seeing an image in the newspaper

> **B.** Overhearing the conversations of a stranger

> **C.** Receiving suggestions from other people

2 Of the sources of ideas that Jacqueline Wilson mentions, which occurs the least frequently? How can you tell this?

3 From reading the whole blog, decide which of these statements are true and which are false. Be ready to discuss and justify your decision on each statement.

> **A.** The most frequent question is what do your characters look like.

> **B.** Everyone gets their ideas in different ways.

> **C.** Recording ideas on paper will help you later.

> **D.** Staring at a blank screen helps with the writing process.

> **E.** Writing very quickly can sometimes be a helpful technique.

> **F.** Editors are like teachers, but more demanding.

> **G.** Once you have lots of good ideas on paper, rewriting isn't usually necessary.

Advanced reading skills

1 Look again at the section 'How to Create Characters'. Here, Jacqueline Wilson writes: 'Did you ever have imaginary friends when you were little?'

In your own words, explain how this use of a question to the reader helps her to communicate her advice in this section.

2 In some parts of her blog, Jacqueline Wilson uses exclamation marks at the end of sentences, for example: 'This is the difficult bit!'

Explain what effect the use of an exclamation mark has here.

3 Jacqueline Wilson clearly wants to end her stories in an interesting way. In your own words, explain what she tries to do with the endings of her stories.

4 Look at how Jacqueline Wilson uses language in her blog. Focus on this sentence:

> **A.** So, let's say you've taken your time over your ending and are pleased with your story.

She could instead have written it like this to communicate the same meaning:

> **B.** Let us assume that you have deliberated over your ending and are satisfied with your story.

What differences do you notice between versions A and B? Use these prompts for a detailed response to the writer's language choices:

- Version A starts with the word 'So'. The effect of this is…
- Version A uses contracted forms of words ('let's' and 'you've' rather than 'let us' and 'you have'). The effect of this is…
- Version A uses 'say' rather than 'assume' and 'taken your time' rather than 'deliberated'. The effect of this is…
- Overall, I prefer version A/B because…

5.2 Letter to Joan Lancaster by C. S. Lewis, 1956

As the author of the classic children's book *The Lion, the Witch and the Wardrobe*, C. S. Lewis received many letters from young fans of his fantasy series *The Chronicles of Narnia*. Here is his reply to a letter he received from an American girl called Joan Lancaster. Joan had sent C. S. Lewis a piece of her own creative writing about a 'wonderful night' and in his reply he comments on this as well as giving some writing advice. As you read the letter, think about how helpful you find C. S. Lewis' advice.

Source text 5.2

WORD BANK

Wordsworth William Wordsworth, an English poet

Prelude an autobiographical poem by William Wordsworth

The Kilns,
Headington Quarry,
Oxford
26 June 1956

Dear Joan–

Thanks for your letter of the 3rd. You describe your Wonderful Night v. well. That is, you describe the place and the people and the night and the feeling of it all, very well — but not the *thing* itself — the setting but not the jewel. And no wonder! **Wordsworth**
5   often does just the same. His *Prelude* (you're bound to read it about 10 years hence. Don't try it now, or you'll only spoil it for

later reading) is full of moments in which everything except the *thing* itself is described. If you become a writer you'll be trying to describe the *thing* all your life: and lucky if, out of dozens of
10 books, one or two sentences, just for a moment, come near to getting it across.

About *amn't I*, *aren't I* and *am I not*, of course there are no right or wrong answers about language in the sense in which there are right and wrong answers in Arithmetic. "Good English" is
15 whatever educated people talk; so that what is good in one place or time would not be so in another. *Amn't I* was good 50 years ago in the North of Ireland where I was brought up, but bad in Southern England. *Aren't I* would have been hideously bad in Ireland but very good in England. And of course I just don't know which (if either)
20 is good in modern Florida. Don't take any notice of teachers and textbooks in such matters. Nor of logic. It is good to say "more than one passenger was hurt," although *more than one* equals at least two and therefore logically the verb ought to be plural *were* not singular *was*!

25 What really matters is:–

1. Always try to use the language so as to make quite clear what you mean and make sure your sentence couldn't mean anything else.

2. Always prefer the plain direct word to the long, vague one.
30 Don't *implement* promises, but *keep* them.

3. Never use abstract nouns when concrete ones will do. If you mean "More people died" don't say "Mortality rose."

4. In writing. Don't use adjectives which merely tell us how you want us to feel about the thing you are describing. I mean,
35 instead of telling us a thing was "terrible," describe it so that we'll be terrified. Don't say it was "delightful"; make *us* say "delightful" when we've read the description. You see, all those words (horrifying, wonderful, hideous, exquisite) are only like saying to your readers, "Please will you do my job for me."

40 5. Don't use words too big for the subject. Don't say "infinitely" when you mean "very"; otherwise you'll have no word left when you want to talk about something *really* infinite.

Thanks for the photos. You and **Aslan** both look v. well. I hope you'll like your new home.

45 With love
yours
C. S. Lewis

WORD BANK

Aslan a powerful lion character in C. S. Lewis' series *The Chronicles of Narnia* (possibly also the name of Jean's pet)

Basic reading skills

1 Re-read the opening paragraph of the letter.

    a What four things does C. S. Lewis say Joan has described very well?

    b What does C. S. Lewis say Joan hasn't described?

    c Which other writer does the same thing according to C. S. Lewis?

2 Based on the text, decide whether the following statements are true or false.

> Only people in Southern England speak 'Good English'.

> There is no such thing as 'Good English'.

> 'Good English' changes over time.

> 'Good English' is the language spoken by educated people.

3 Why does C. S. Lewis recommend using the word 'keep' instead of 'implement'?

4 Find a phrase or sentence in the text that suggests C. S. Lewis likes writing that appeals to his readers' emotions.

5 Look at the sentence: 'Don't use words too big for the subject.' Decide which of the following statements match what the writer is suggesting:

> Don't use big words because people don't like them.

> Use words as precisely as you can.

> Big words confuse people.

> Sometimes it is worth using simpler words so that the more complex ones will have a real impact when you use them.

Advanced reading skills

1 Look again at the sentence: 'If you become a writer you'll be trying to describe the *thing* all your life: and lucky if, out of dozens of books, one or two sentences, just for a moment, come near to getting it across.'

    a What might 'the thing' C. S. Lewis writes about be in this instance?

    b What does this sentence suggest about the challenges of being a writer?

2 Which of the following words do you think best describes the tone of C. S. Lewis' letter? Justify your choice with reference to the text.

stern

gentle

kind

generous

uncertain

aloof

3a C. S. Lewis uses different types of punctuation in the letter. Find examples of the following and for each one, explain the effect the punctuation creates:

- dash
- exclamation mark
- colon
- quotation marks.

3b C. S. Lewis also uses italics in places. Explain why you think he does this. Remember to give examples from the text to support your explanation.

4 Explore which pieces of advice in the letter you find most helpful and explain why they might help you with your own writing.

Key term

pseudonym a false
name

5.3 *The Life of Charlotte Brontë* by Elizabeth Gaskell, 1857

Charlotte Brontë was a 19th-century author, whose best-known novel *Jane Eyre* was first published under the **pseudonym** Currer Bell. Charlotte Brontë died at the age of thirty-eight. Her fellow novelist Elizabeth Gaskell wrote the biography *The Life of Charlotte Brontë*, which was first published in 1857, two years after her premature death. As you read the following extract, think about the impression it gives you of Charlotte Brontë.

Source text 5.3

WORD BANK

venture a project, typically one that involves risk

acute severe or intense

befell happened to

manifest show it clearly

stoicism the endurance of pain or hardship without the display of feelings and without complaint

tardy slow to act or respond

borne endured

ill-success lack of success

adverse bad

The sisters had kept the knowledge of their literary **ventures** from their father, fearing to increase their own anxieties and disappointment by witnessing his; for he took an **acute** interest in all that **befell** his children, and his own tendency had been
5 towards literature in the days when he was young and hopeful. It was true he did not much **manifest** his feelings in words; he would have thought that he was prepared for disappointment as the lot of man, and that he could have met it with **stoicism**; but words are poor and **tardy** interpreters of feelings to those who love one
10 another, and his daughters knew how he would have **borne ill-success** worse for them than for himself. So they did not tell him what they were undertaking. He says now that he suspected it all along, but his suspicions could take no exact form, as all he was certain of was, that his children were perpetually writing — and
15 not writing letters. We have seen how the communications from their publishers were received "under cover to Miss Brontë." Once, Charlotte told me, they overheard the postman meeting Mr. Brontë, as the latter was leaving the house, and inquiring from the parson where one Currer Bell could be living, to which Mr. Brontë replied
20 that there was no such person in the parish. [...]

Now, however, when the demand for the work had assured success to "Jane Eyre," her sisters urged Charlotte to tell their father of its publication. She accordingly went into his study one afternoon after his early dinner, carrying with her a copy of the
25 book, and one or two reviews, taking care to include a notice **adverse** to it.

She informed me that something like the following conversation took place between her and him. (I wrote down her words the day after I heard them; and I am pretty sure they are quite accurate.)
30 "Papa, I've been writing a book."

"Have you, my dear?"

"Yes, and I want you to read it."

"I am afraid it will try my eyes too much."

"But it is not in manuscript: it is printed."

35 "My dear! you've never thought of the expense it will be! It will be almost sure to be a loss, for how can you get a book sold? No one knows you or your name."

"But, papa, I don't think it will be a loss; no more will you, if you will just let me read you a review or two, and tell you more about it."

40 So she sate down and read some of the reviews to her father; and then, giving him the copy of "Jane Eyre" that she intended for him, she left him to read it. When he came in to tea, he said, "Girls, do you know Charlotte has been writing a book, and it is much better than likely?"

45 But while the existence of Currer Bell, the author, was like a piece of a dream to the quiet inhabitants of **Haworth Parsonage**, who went on with their uniform household life — their cares for their brother being its only variety — the whole reading-world of England was in a **ferment** to discover the unknown author. Even 50 the publishers of "Jane Eyre" were ignorant whether Currer Bell was a real or an assumed name — whether it belonged to a man or a woman. In every town people sought out the list of their friends and acquaintances, and turned away in disappointment. No one they knew had genius enough to be the author.

WORD BANK

Haworth Parsonage
the church house in Haworth, the Yorkshire village where the Brontë family lived

ferment an excited or agitated condition

Basic reading skills

1 Why did Charlotte Brontë and her sisters keep their writing a secret from their father?

2 Pick out a quotation that suggests that Charlotte Brontë's father had been interested in writing stories when he was younger.

3a What did the postman ask Mr Brontë?

3b What did Mr Brontë reply?

4 Why did Charlotte Brontë finally decide to tell her father that she had published a novel?

5 Look again at the dialogue between Charlotte and her father which begins, "Papa, I've been writing a book." Using your own words, summarize Mr Brontë's response to the news Charlotte gives him.

6 Look again at the final sentence: 'No one they knew had genius enough to be the author.' What does this suggest about people's opinions of *Jane Eyre*?

Advanced reading skills

1 *The Life of Charlotte Brontë* was first published in 1857. Pick out one example of dialogue that you think best indicates the time this book was written. Explain your choice.

2 The author writes of Mr Brontë, 'his daughters knew how he would have borne ill-success worse for them than for himself'. Explain what you think this means in your own words.

3 Which of the following words would you use to describe Mr Brontë's character? Justify your choices with reference to the text.

cautious   caring   anxious   hopeful   shy

unemotional   suspicious   modest   proud   calm

4 What impression do you get of Charlotte Brontë from this extract? In your answer you should comment on:

- her actions and the decisions she makes

- her conversation with her father and what it suggests about her

- the way the writer describes the public's reaction to her novel *Jane Eyre*.

Extended reading

Compare how two of the texts you have read in this section convey the skills you need to be a writer. Think about:

- the information each text gives about writers and writing
- what this suggests about the skills needed to be a writer
- the purpose of each text and how effectively it achieves this.

Extended writing

Choose one of the authors covered in this section (Dame Jacqueline Wilson, C. S. Lewis or Charlotte Brontë) and write a letter to them asking for their writing advice. In your letter you should:

- follow the conventions for the format of a letter, using an appropriate greeting and ending
- explain why you are writing to them
- outline any aspects of your writing that you would like to improve
- use an appropriate tone.

Remember to check the spelling, punctuation and grammar of your writing.

Early bird

List your own top ten tips for becoming a better writer. Decide which ones you need to prioritize in your own writing.

Source texts table

Text	Genre	Date
6.1 *Travels in West Africa* by Mary Kingsley	Eyewitness account	1897
6.2 'Chimpanzees – Bridging the gap' by Jane Goodall	Essay	1993
6.3 'Penguin swims 5,000 miles every year for reunion with the man who saved his life' by Alison Lynch	Newspaper article	2016

Big picture

On our planet, there are millions of species of animals of which human beings are only one. Humans often see themselves as being superior to animals. Do you agree with this point of view? Explain why or why not.

In this section you will read three texts that explore our relationships with animals: an extract from a piece of 19th-century travel writing describing the author's encounter with gorillas in West Africa; an extract from an essay written by the scientist Jane Goodall exploring the similarities between humans and chimpanzees; and a newspaper article about a penguin who swims 5,000 miles every year to meet the man who saved his life.

Skills

- Understand the meaning of a text

- Make inferences and refer to evidence in a text

- Comment on a writer's use of language and structure (including sensory language, **imagery**, quotations, openings and endings)

- Compare texts

- Practise writing an eyewitness account, drawing on techniques and ideas explored in your reading

Before reading

Key term

imagery writing which creates a picture or appeals to other senses; this includes simile, metaphor and personification and the use of vivid verbs, nouns, adjectives and adverbs

1   Think back on your own animal encounters. This might be a relationship with a family pet or a visit to the zoo to see wild animals. How have these experiences shaped your views about animals?

2   Some people believe that intelligent animals such as gorillas and chimpanzees should be given the same rights as humans. Give two reasons why you think this would be a good idea and one reason against this proposal.

6.1 *Travels in West Africa* by Mary Kingsley, 1897

Mary Kingsley was a scientist and explorer who travelled extensively in West Africa in the late 19th century. In the following extract from *Travels in West Africa*, she describes an encounter with a group of five gorillas in the wild. As you read, think about the impression you get of Mary Kingsley's feelings about this first-hand experience.

Source text 6.1

WORD BANK

plantains a variety of banana

depredations actions that involve plundering or damaging something

haunches the top part of the thighs

Wiki one of Mary Kingsley's companions on her expedition

I saw before me some thirty yards off, busily employed in pulling down **plantains**, and other **depredations**, five gorillas: one old male, one young male, and three females. One of these had clinging to her a young fellow, with beautiful wavy black hair with
5 just a kink in it. The big male was crouching on his **haunches**, with his long arms hanging down on either side, with the backs of his hands on the ground, the palms upwards. The elder lady was tearing to pieces and eating a pine-apple, while the others were at the plantains destroying more than they ate.

10   They kept up a sort of a whinnying, chattering noise, quite different from the sound I have heard gorillas give when enraged, or from the one you can hear them giving when they are what the natives call "dancing" at night. I noticed that their reach of arm was immense, and that when they went from one tree to another,
15 they squattered across the open ground in a most inelegant style, dragging their long arms with the knuckles downwards. I should think the big male and female were over six feet each. The others would be from four to five. I put out my hand and laid it on **Wiki**'s gun to prevent him from firing, and he, thinking I was going to fire,
20 gripped my wrist.

    I watched the gorillas with great interest for a few seconds, until I heard Wiki make a peculiar small sound, and looking at him saw his face was working in an awful way as he clutched his throat with his hand violently.

25   Heavens! think I, this gentleman's going to have a fit; it's lost we are entirely this time. He rolled his head to and fro, and then buried his face into a heap of dried rubbish at the foot of a plantain stem, clasped his hands over it, and gave an explosive sneeze. The gorillas let go all, raised themselves up for a second, gave a quaint sound
30 between a bark and a howl, and then the ladies and the young gentleman started home. The old male rose to his full height (it struck me at the time this was a matter of ten feet at least, but for scientific purposes allowance must be made for a lady's emotions) and looked straight towards us, or rather towards where that sound

WORD BANK

paroxysm a sudden outburst

celerity swiftness of movement

35 came from. Wiki went off into a **paroxysm** of falsetto sneezes the like of which I have never heard; nor evidently had the gorilla, who […] went off after his family with a **celerity** that was amazing the moment he touched the forest, and disappeared as they had, swinging himself along through it from bough to bough, in a
40 way that convinced me that, given the necessity of getting about in tropical forests, man has made a mistake in getting his arms shortened. I have seen many wild animals in their native wilds, but never have I seen anything to equal gorillas going through bush; it is a graceful, powerful, superbly perfect hand-trapeze performance.

Basic reading skills

1   Look again at the first paragraph. Summarize what the gorillas are doing when Mary Kingsley first spots them.

2a Now look at the second paragraph. Note down three facts that you learn about the gorillas from this paragraph.

2b Mary Kingsley says the gorillas 'squattered across the open ground in a most inelegant style'. Using your own words, provide a definition for the word 'squattered'.

3   How can you tell that Mary Kingsley is worried that Wiki will shoot the gorillas?

4   What happens to disturb the gorillas?

5 Pick one of the following words to describe the gorillas' reaction to the disturbance. Give reasons for your choice.

 amazed

frightened

 excited

grateful

forgetful

Advanced reading skills

1 Write down three words which you think best describe the gorillas that Mary Kingsley observes. Then select a quotation that you think best illustrates each word.

2 Does Mary Kingsley appear to be scared of the gorillas? In a sentence, explain why or why not. Use an example from the text to support your answer.

3 In order to describe to the reader what her encounter with gorillas was like, Mary Kingsley uses words and phrases relating to different senses. Pick out a quotation to show how she uses each of these senses and explain the effect this creates:

■ sight

■ sound

■ touch.

4 This text was written in the late 19th century. Look at the following sentence and comment on how this suggests when the text was written: 'Heavens! think I, this gentleman's going to have a fit; it's lost we are entirely this time.'

In your answer you should comment on:

■ vocabulary choice   ■ word order

■ sentence form   ■ use of punctuation.

5 Find an example of humour in the text and explain what it suggests about Kingsley's personality.

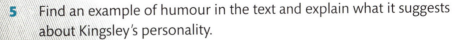

6.2 'Chimpanzees – Bridging the gap' by Jane Goodall, 1993

Jane Goodall is a scientist and animal rights campaigner. In this essay, she explores the similarities between human beings and chimpanzees. As you read, think about the impression the writer gives you about her views and feelings towards chimpanzees.

Source text 6.2

WORD BANK

Gombe the north-eastern part of Nigeria

Mahale Mountains a national park in Tanzania

Chimpanzees can live more than fifty years. Infants suckle and are carried by their mothers for five years. And then, even when the next infant is born, the elder child travels with his or her mother for another three or four years and continues to spend a good deal of
5 time with her thereafter. The ties between family members are close, affectionate and supportive, and typically endure throughout life. Learning is important in the individual life cycle. Chimpanzees, like humans, can learn by observation and imitation, which means that if a new adaptive pattern is 'invented' by a particular individual, it
10 can be passed on to the next generation. Thus we find that while the various chimpanzee groups that have been studied in different parts of Africa have many behaviours in common, they also have their own distinctive traditions. This is particularly well documented with respect to tool-using and tool-making behaviours. Chimpanzees
15 use more objects as tools for a greater variety of purposes than any creature except ourselves and each population has its own tool-using cultures. For example, the **Gombe** chimpanzees use long, straight sticks from which the bark has been peeled to extract army ants from their nests; 100 miles to the south, in the **Mahale Mountains**,
20 there are plenty of the same ants, but they are not eaten by the chimpanzees. The Mahale chimpanzees use small twigs to extract carpenter ants from their nests in tree branches; these ants, though present, are not eaten at Gombe. And no East African chimpanzee has been seen to open hard-shelled fruits with the hammer and
25 anvil technique that is part of the culture of chimpanzee groups in West Africa.

  The postures and gestures with which chimpanzees communicate – such as kissing, embracing, holding hands, patting one another on the back, swaggering, punching, hair-pulling, tickling – are
30 not only uncannily like many of our own, but are used in similar contexts and clearly have similar meanings. Two friends may greet with an embrace and a fearful individual may be calmed by a touch, whether they be chimpanzees or humans. Chimpanzees are capable of sophisticated co-operation and complex social manipulation. Like
35 us, they have a dark side to their nature: they can be brutal, they are

WORD BANK

territorial a territorial
animal guards and
defends an area of
land it believes to be
its own

altruism behaviour
of an animal that
benefits another at its
own expense

generalisation
the action of
generalizing, that
is, forming general
concepts by inferring
from specific cases

abstraction the quality
of dealing with ideas
rather than events

concept-forming the
development of ideas

cognitive relating to
thinking

aggressively **territorial**, sometimes they even engage in a primitive type of warfare. But they also show a variety of helping and caregiving behaviours and are capable of true **altruism**. [...]

40 Our own success as a species (if we measure success by the extent to which we have spread across the world and altered the environment to suit our immediate purposes) has been due entirely to the explosive development of the human brain. Our intellectual abilities are so much more sophisticated than those of even the most gifted chimpanzees that early attempts made by scientists to describe 45 the similarity of mental process in humans and chimpanzees were largely met with ridicule or outrage. Gradually, however, evidence for sophisticated mental performances in the apes has become ever more convincing. There is proof that they can solve simple problems through process of reasoning and insight. They can plan 50 for the immediate future. The language acquisition experiments have demonstrated that they have powers of **generalisation**, **abstraction** and **concept-forming** along with the ability to understand and use abstract symbols in communication. And they clearly have some kind of self-concept.

55 It is all a little humbling, for these **cognitive** abilities used to be considered unique to humans: we are not, after all, quite as different from the rest of the animal kingdom as we used to think. The line dividing 'man' from 'beast' has become increasingly blurred. The chimpanzees, 60 and the other great apes, form a living bridge between 'us' and 'them', and this knowledge forces us to re-evaluate our relationship with the rest of the animal kingdom, particularly 65 with the great apes. In what terms should we think of these beings, nonhuman yet possessing so very many human-like characteristics? How should we treat them?

70 Surely we should treat them with the same consideration and kindness as we show to other humans; and as we recognise human rights, so too should we recognise the rights of the great 75 apes?

Basic reading skills

1 Re-read the opening paragraph.

a List two facts about chimpanzee children.

b Choose three of the following words to describe the relationship between different members of a chimpanzee family:

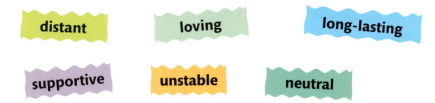

distant   loving   long-lasting

supportive   unstable   neutral

c 'Chimpanzees, like humans, can learn by observation and imitation.' Using your own words, explain what this means.

d What do the Gombe chimpanzees use tools to do?

e What do the chimpanzees of West Africa use tools to do?

2 Jane Goodall is a scientist.

a Pick out three examples of scientific language that you can find in the essay.

b Explain what effect this use of scientific language has on you as a reader.

3 Find an example of chimpanzee behaviour that suggests the 'dark side to their nature'.

4 Pick out three more similarities between humans and chimpanzees.

5 What does the writer suggest is responsible for the human race's success as a species?

Advanced reading skills

Key term

biased a biased opinion is one based on one viewpoint which doesn't examine the facts fairly

1 Jane Goodall writes that the postures and gestures that chimpanzees use to communicate are 'uncannily' like many of our own. Explain what the word 'uncannily' means here and why you think the writer has chosen to use this word.

2 Choose one sentence from the essay that you think best sums up the writer's attitude to chimpanzees. Write it down and then explain why you have chosen it.

3 Summarize in a paragraph the argument Jane Goodall presents in this essay.

4 Read one student's comment about the essay.

I think the writer of this article is **biased**.

Explain what this student means and whether you agree or disagree with their statement. Refer to the text to support your view.

6.3 'Penguin swims 5,000 miles every year for reunion with the man who saved his life' by Alison Lynch, 2016

The following newspaper article was first published in the *Metro* newspaper and online on 9 March 2016 and is about a penguin who swims 5,000 miles every year to meet the man who saved his life. As you read, think about the impression the writer gives you of this event.

Source text 6.3

Today's most heartwarming story is brought to you from a beach in Brazil.

It's the story of a South American Magellanic penguin who swims 5,000 miles each year to be reunited with the man who saved his life.

Retired bricklayer and part time fisherman Joao Pereira de Souza, 71, who lives in an island village just outside Rio de Janeiro, Brazil, found
5 the tiny penguin, covered in oil and close to death, lying on rocks on his local beach in 2011.

Joao cleaned the oil off the penguin's feathers and fed him a daily diet of fish to build his strength. He named him Dindim.

After a week, he tried to release the penguin back into the sea. But, the
10 bird wouldn't leave. 'He stayed with me for 11 months and then, just after he changed his coat with new feathers, he disappeared,' Joao recalls.

And, just a few months later, Dindim was back. He spotted the fisherman on the beach one day and followed him home.

For the past five years, Dindim has spent eight months of the year
15 with Joao and is believed to spend the rest of the time breeding off the coast of Argentina and Chile.

It's thought he swims up to 5,000 miles each year to be reunited with the man who saved his life.

'I love the penguin like it's my own child and I believe the penguin
20 loves me,' Joao told Globo TV.

'No one else is allowed to touch him. He pecks them if they do. He lays on my lap, lets me give him showers, allows me to feed him sardines and to pick him up.

'Everyone said he wouldn't return but he has been coming back to
25 visit me for the past four years.

'He arrives in June and leaves to go home in February and every year he becomes more affectionate as he appears even happier to see me.'

Biologist Professor Krajewski, who interviewed the fisherman for Globo TV, told *The Independent*: 'I have never seen anything like
30 this before. I think the penguin believes Joao is part of his family and probably a penguin as well.

'When he sees him he wags his tail like a dog and honks with delight.'
And, just like that, the world seems a kinder place again.

Basic reading skills

1   What is the name of the fisherman who saved the penguin's life?

2   How did the fisherman save the penguin?

3   What name did the fisherman give to the penguin?

4   How long did the penguin first stay with the fisherman?

5   The fisherman says, 'I love the penguin like it's my own child and I believe the penguin loves me.' Pick out two quotations from the article that support this statement.

6   How does the writer suggest the relationship between the penguin and the man is so unusual?

7   What impression do you get of the writer's view of this news story? Support your answer with reference to the text.

Advanced reading skills

Key term

direct speech when the words a person has spoken are relayed to the reader exactly, using speech marks

1   Look at the opening sentence of the article. How does it make the reader want to read on?

2   Newspapers and online news sites compete with each other for reader attention and page clicks. Find a piece of evidence from the article that suggests this news story has been covered by other media outlets, for example, newspapers and television channels.

3   Read this comment on the text and decide whether you agree or disagree with it: 'This article isn't really news.'

    Give your response to this comment, referring to the text to support your view.

4   The writer has included **direct speech** from two people in the article.

    a Pick out the two people quoted in the article. Why do you think the writer has chosen to include their voices in this news story?

    b Who else might the writer have chosen to interview and why?

5   Look again at the last line of the newspaper article. Explain why you think the writer has chosen to end the article in this way and how it might affect the readers.

Extended reading

Re-read Mary Kingsley's eyewitness account and the essay by Jane Goodall in order to answer the following question.

Compare the two writers' views about great apes such as gorillas and chimpanzees.

In your answer, you could:

■   compare the views they present, identifying any similarities and differences between these

■   compare the methods the writers use to convey their ideas

■   explore your own thoughts and responses to these as a reader

■   support your ideas with references to both texts.

Extended writing

Write an eyewitness account describing a memorable encounter with an animal. This could be based on a real experience you have had. In your eyewitness account you should:

- convey your attitude towards the animal and your feelings about the encounter

- make language choices that help the reader to share the experience, for example, by using imagery, sensory detail and **onomatopoeia**.

Remember to check the spelling, punctuation and grammar of your writing.

Key term

onomatopoeia words which imitate the sounds they represent

Early bird

The collective noun for a flock of goldfinches is a 'charm of goldfinches'. Invent your own collective nouns for different species of animals. Try to choose words that convey the characteristics of the different animals.

The frontiers of science

Source texts table

Texts	Genre	Date
7.1 'The development of X-rays' by R. A. Gregory	Magazine article	1896
7.2 'Testing the first atomic bomb' by Richard Feynman	Autobiography	1985
7.3 'Questioning the universe' by Professor Stephen Hawking	Speech	2008

Big picture

From the discovery of X-rays to the search for alien life, science is always pushing at the frontiers of the possible. The discoveries that scientists have made have transformed our lives. Do you think most of these discoveries have brought improvements or have they brought new dangers?

In this section you will read three non-fiction texts that explore scientific progress: a 19th-century magazine article about the discovery of X-rays; an extract from a 20th-century autobiography written by the American scientist Richard Feynman in which he describes the test of the first atomic bomb; and an extract from a speech given by Professor Stephen Hawking in which he explores the questions that 21st-century scientists are still investigating.

Skills

Key term

tone a manner of expression in speech or writing

- Understand the meaning of a text
- Make inferences and refer to evidence in a text
- Comment on a writer's use of language and structure (including **tone**, formality, paragraphing and openings)
- Explore the techniques used by a writer to communicate views and ideas
- Practise writing a speech, drawing on techniques and ideas explored in your reading

Before reading

1 Look at the following scientific achievements and inventions:

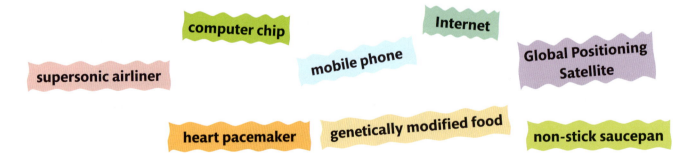

computer chip

Internet

mobile phone

Global Positioning Satellite

supersonic airliner

heart pacemaker

genetically modified food

non-stick saucepan

a Which do you think are the most important? Which are the least? Rank these scientific achievements and inventions in order from the most important to the least.

b Give reasons to support your choice of the most important achievement.

c Give reasons to support your choice of the least important achievement.

2 Add another important scientific achievement or invention to the list. Write a paragraph explaining why you think its impact on the world has been significant.

7.1 'The discovery of X-rays' by R. A. Gregory, 1896

The following article was first published in the 19th-century magazine *The Leisure Hour*. The journalist R. A. Gregory informs readers about the discovery of X-rays by the German scientist Professor Wilhelm Röntgen, although in the article they are just referred to as a kind of 'light-ray', as the term 'X-ray' was not used until later. As you read, think about how the journalist explains what X-rays are. Has it helped your understanding of them?

Source text 7.1

WORD BANK

lo an archaic word meaning 'see' or 'behold'

Marburg University a university in Germany

exemplifies is an example of something

misnomer an unsuitable name; a word or phrase that does not suit the person or thing it describes

opaque not transparent

SCIENCE advances by bringing into view facts and phenomena previously unknown. Galileo turns his simple telescope towards the heavens, and **lo**! thousands of stars beyond the grasp of the unaided vision are revealed;
5 the microscope is invented, and by its aid an unseen universe, the inhabitants of which are far more numerous than the stars in heaven, is made known. In neither case were new worlds or beings created, the extension of knowledge being but a consequence of the improved powers of seeing. The
10 recent development of photography, associated with the name of Professor Röntgen, of **Marburg University, exemplifies** this idea. It has been discovered that a kind of light-rays – if the term be not a **misnomer** – can be produced which will pass through **opaque** substances, such as wood and aluminium, more easily
15 than through glass, and that these rays can produce an effect upon a sensitised surface such as that of a photographic plate. Further, the rays will pass through flesh more easily than through bone, so that if a hand is held in front of a source emitting them, the bones of the hand can be seen distinctly in the shadow
20 thrown. The facts seem so simple that it is difficult to believe that they have only been acquired after many years of patient work. [...]
 Professor Röntgen has produced many electric shadows, or shadowgraphs, in the same way, by taking advantage of the fact that different substances allow the new rays to pass through

←

WORD BANK

bobbin a cylinder on which wire or thread is wound

permeable allowing substances to pass through

excited charged, to cause a reaction

ubiquitous found everywhere

25 them with different facilities. He has photographed wire wound around a **bobbin**, the wire stopping the rays while the wood of the bobbin was **permeable** to them. A set of metal weights in a wooden box, when placed in the path of the rays, produced a picture of the weights alone; and a compass card and magnetic
30 needle, completely enclosed in a case, was photographed [...]. Other objects have been similarly experimented upon, the object in each case being between an electrically **excited** vacuum tube and a photographic plate. [...]

35 As to the possibilities of the new photography, it will be consoling to most people to know that the **ubiquitous** amateur photographer will not be able to obtain snap-shots of their skeletons as they walk along the street. Only by means of the radiations obtained electrically in the manner described have
40 the new shadowgraphs yet been made. In surgery, the method should undoubtedly prove useful, for, as will be manifest from the accompanying illustrations of human hands, slight deformations of bones, or the nature of a fracture, could easily be located by means of such pictures. Already the process has been utilised to
45 show the position of a small revolver bullet in a man's hand; to point out the destroyed parts in a diseased thigh-bone, and to photograph a stone in the bladder of a living person; and there is every reason to believe that blow-holes and flaws concealed in the interior of metal structures could be revealed by it. We may,
50 therefore, confidently expect, now that the applications of the method have been indicated, that full advantage will be taken of them.

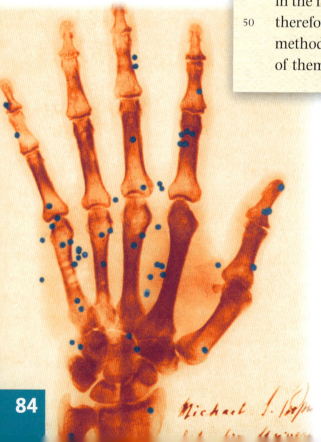

Basic reading skills

1   In the first paragraph, the writer names two other scientific advances apart from the discovery of X-rays. List both of these advances.

2   Are the following statements true or false?

>   **A.** Professor Röntgen works at Marburg University.

>   **B.** He has been unable to take photographs using X-rays.

>   **C.** X-rays travel through flesh more easily than bone.

>   **D.** The writer thinks X-rays will help doctors and surgeons.

3   The writer refers to 'shadowgraphs'. Based on your understanding of the text, write a definition for this term.

4   Look again at the final paragraph.

   a Name one development that the writer predicts X-rays will helpfully be used for.

   b Name one development that the writer does not expect X-rays to be used for.

Advanced reading skills

1   Look again at the first sentence of the article: 'Science advances by bringing into view facts and phenomena previously unknown.' Explain why you think the writer has chosen to begin the article with this sentence. Do you think it is an effective opening? Give reasons for your answer.

Key term

sentence forms
sentence types (that is, statement, question, command, exclamation) and sentence structures (that is, single, minor, multi-clause)

2   Look again at the opening paragraph.

   a Pick out three quotations that refer to sight or seeing.

   b Explain why you think the writer has chosen to include these references.

3   In the first paragraph, the journalist writes: 'It has been discovered that a kind of light-rays – if the term be not a misnomer – can be produced which will pass through opaque substances...' Explain why the choice of the word 'misnomer' is an appropriate one.

4   Read the following student's comment on the text:

   The writer is impressed by Professor Röntgen's discovery.

   Explain whether you agree or disagree with this statement. Refer to evidence from the text to support your view.

5   Look at the first and final paragraphs of the article. What links can you find between these two paragraphs, and what effect do these create?

6   If you were writing this article for a magazine today, how would you make the text more interesting for a modern-day reader? Think about:

   ■   the information presented and the language used to convey this

   ■   your choice of **sentence forms** and the way you could structure the article.

   Rewrite the article in a shorter, more direct way.

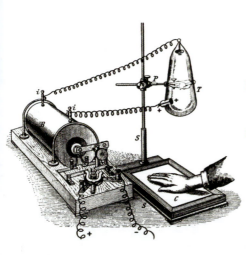

7.2 'Testing the first atomic bomb' by Richard Feynman, 1985

The following extract is taken from *Surely You're Joking, Mr Feynman!*, a autobiography by the Nobel-Prize-winning scientist Richard Feynman. Following the outbreak of the Second World War, the US government recruited a team of scientists to develop the atomic bomb. Richard Feynman was one of these scientists. Here, he describes witnessing the test explosion of the first atomic bomb in 1945.

Source text 7.2

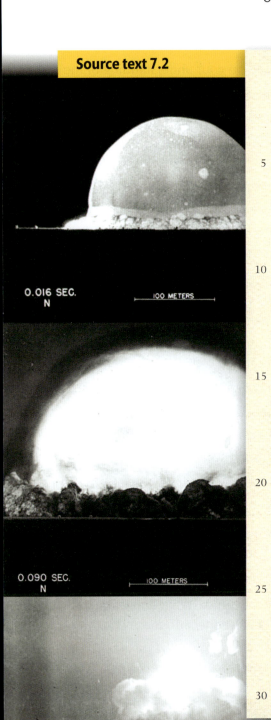

I flew back, and I arrived *just* when the buses were leaving, so I went straight out to the site and we waited out there, twenty miles away. We had a radio, and they were supposed to tell us when the thing was going to go off and so forth, but the radio wouldn't work,
5 so we never knew what was happening. But just a few minutes before it was supposed to go off the radio started to work, and they told us there was twenty seconds or something to go, for people who were far away like we were. Others were closer, six miles away.

They gave out dark glasses that you could watch it with. Dark
10 glasses! Twenty miles away, you couldn't see a damn thing through dark glasses. So I figured the only thing that could really hurt your eyes (bright light can never hurt your eyes) is ultraviolet light. I got behind a truck windshield, because the ultraviolet can't go through glass, so that would be safe, and so I could *see* the damn thing.

15 Time comes, and this *tremendous* flash out there is so bright that I duck, and I see this purple splotch on the floor of the truck. I said, "That's not it. That's an after-image." So I look back up, and I see this white light changing into yellow and then into orange. Clouds form and disappear again—from the compression and the
20 expansion of the shock wave.

Finally, a big ball of orange, the center that was so bright, becomes a ball of orange that starts to rise and billow a little bit and get a little black around the edges, and then you see it's a big ball of smoke with flashes on the inside of the fire going out, the heat.

25 All this took about one minute. It was a series from bright to dark, and I had *seen* it. I am about the only guy who actually looked at the damn thing—the first Trinity test. Everybody else had dark glasses, and the people at six miles couldn't see it because they were all told to lie on the floor. I'm probably the only guy who saw it with
30 the human eye.

Finally, after about a minute and a half, there's suddenly a tremendous noise—BANG, and then a rumble, like thunder—and that's what convinced me. Nobody had said a word during this whole thing. We were all just watching quietly. But this sound
35   released everybody—released me particularly because the solidity of the sound at that distance meant that it had really worked.

The man standing next to me said, "What's that?"

I said, "That was the bomb." [...]

After the thing went off, there was tremendous excitement at
40   Los Alamos. Everybody had parties, we all ran around. I sat on the end of a jeep and beat drums and so on. But one man I remember, Bob Wilson, was just sitting there moping.

I said, "What are you moping about?"

He said, "It's a terrible thing that we made."
45   I said, "But you started it. You got us into it."

You see, what happened to me—what happened to the rest of us—is we *started* for a good reason, then you're working very hard to accomplish something and it's a pleasure, it's excitement. And you stop thinking, you know; you just *stop*. So Bob Wilson was the
50   only one who was still thinking about it, at that moment.

100 METERS

100 METERS

Basic reading skills

1   How far away was Richard Feynman from the test site when the atomic bomb was tested?

2   How close does Richard Feynman say other people were to the test site?

3   Why does Richard Feynman decide not to wear dark glasses to watch the test?

4   What does Richard Feynman do to protect his eyes?

5   'I'm probably the only guy who saw it with the human eye.' List two facts that Richard Feynman gives to support this statement.

6   Which of the following events seems to prompt the people watching the test to start talking?

   ■   The initial flash of the explosion

   ■   The sound of the bang

   ■   The shock wave

7   Summarize how Bob Wilson appears to feel about the atomic bomb.

Advanced reading skills

1 Which of these words best summarizes how Richard Feynman feels during the events of the extract? Write a sentence explaining your choice.

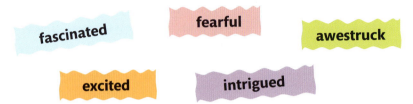

fascinated

fearful

awestruck

excited

intrigued

2 What do you learn about Richard Feynman? Use a spider diagram to record any clues about his personality and character from the extract.

3 Read the section from the paragraph beginning, 'Time comes...' to the paragraph ending '... the solidity of the sound at that distance meant that it had really worked'. Create a timeline to chart the progress of the test explosion. Pick out any quotations that you think are particularly effective in helping you to understand the different stages of the explosion and record these on your timeline.

4 Richard Feynman was known as a great communicator, helping non-scientists to understand scientific theories and achievements. How effectively do you think he explains the test explosion of the first atomic bomb? In your answer you should comment on:

- how he uses **similes** and **metaphors**
- his choice of verb **tenses**
- the descriptive details he includes and the effects these create
- the sentence forms he uses and the effects these create
- the formality of the language he uses.

Key terms

simile a comparison where one thing is compared to another using the words *like* or *as*

metaphor the use of a word or phrase which describes something by likening it to something else

tense the tense of the verb tells you when the action of the verb takes place (present, past or future)

7.3 'Questioning the universe' by Stephen Hawking, 2008

Professor Stephen Hawking is probably the most famous scientist in the world today. In the following extract from a TED Talk he gave in February 2008, Professor Hawking asks some big questions about the universe. As you read, think about these big questions and decide how effectively you think Professor Hawking answers them.

Source text 7.3

WORD BANK

extrapolate draw conclusions from information

SETI search for extra-terrestrial intelligence

There is nothing bigger or older than the universe. The questions I would like to talk about are: one, where did we come from? How did the universe come into being? Are we alone in the universe? Is there alien life out there? What is the future of the human race?

5   Up until the 1920s, everyone thought the universe was essentially static and unchanging in time. Then it was discovered that the universe was expanding. Distant galaxies were moving away from us. This meant they must have been closer together in the past. If we **extrapolate** back, we find we must have all been on

10 top of each other about 15 billion years ago. This was the Big Bang, the beginning of the universe. [...]

   I now turn to the second big question: are we alone, or is there other life in the universe? We believe that life arose spontaneously on the Earth, so it must be possible for life to appear on other

15 suitable planets, of which there seem to be a large number in the galaxy.

   But we don't know how life first appeared. We have two pieces of observational evidence on the probability of life appearing. The first is that we have fossils of algae from 3.5 billion years ago. The

20 Earth was formed 4.6 billion years ago and was probably too hot for about the first half billion years. So life appeared on Earth within half a billion years of it being possible, which is short compared to the 10-billion-year lifetime of a planet of Earth type. This suggests that the probability of life appearing is reasonably high. If it was

25 very low, one would have expected it to take most of the ten billion years available.

   On the other hand, we don't seem to have been visited by aliens. I am discounting the reports of UFOs. Why would they appear only to cranks and weirdos? If there is a government conspiracy to

30 suppress the reports and keep for itself the scientific knowledge the aliens bring, it seems to have been a singularly ineffective policy so far. Furthermore, despite an extensive search by the **SETI** project, we haven't heard any alien television quiz shows. This probably

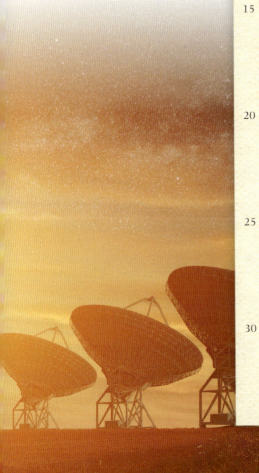

indicates that there are no alien civilizations at our stage of
35　development within a radius of a few hundred light years. Issuing an
insurance policy against abduction by aliens seems a pretty safe bet.

　　This brings me to the last of the big questions: the future of the
human race. If we are the only intelligent beings in the galaxy, we
should make sure we survive and continue. But we are entering
40　an increasingly dangerous period of our history. Our population
and our use of the finite resources of planet Earth are growing
exponentially, along with our technical ability to change the
environment for good or ill. But our genetic code still carries the
selfish and aggressive instincts that were of survival advantage
45　in the past. It will be difficult enough to avoid disaster in the next
hundred years, let alone the next thousand or million.

　　Our only chance of long-term survival is not to remain inward-
looking on planet Earth, but to spread out into space. The answers to
these big questions show that we have made remarkable progress in
50　the last hundred years. But if we want to continue beyond the next
hundred years, our future is in space. That is why I am in favor of
manned — or should I say, personned — space flight.

　　All of my life I have sought to understand the universe and
find answers to these questions. I have been very lucky that my
55　disability has not been a serious handicap. Indeed, it has probably
given me more time than most people to pursue the quest for
knowledge. The ultimate goal is a complete theory of the universe,
and we are making good progress. Thank you for listening.

WORD BANK

exponentially more
and more rapidly

Basic reading skills

1　One of the questions Professor Stephen Hawking says he wants to talk
about is, 'How did the universe come into being?'

　a　List four more questions Professor Stephen Hawking says he wants
to talk about.

　b　Which of these questions interests you the most? Give a reason for
your answer.

2　How long ago does Professor Stephen Hawking say the universe began?

3　Pick out two pieces of evidence Professor Stephen Hawking gives to
support his statement that we don't seem to have been visited by aliens.

4　List two reasons Professor Stephen Hawking gives to support his claim
that we are entering an increasingly dangerous period in our history.

5　What does Professor Stephen Hawking suggest is the best way to ensure
the long-term survival of the human race?

Advanced reading skills

1   Why do you think Professor Stephen Hawking includes so many questions in his talk? Support your explanation with examples of questions from the text.

2   Look at the structure of the talk. In the opening paragraph Professor Stephen Hawking sets out the five questions he wants to talk about. Copy and complete a table like the one below to record which questions he explores in each paragraph.

Paragraph	Question explored
2	
3	
4	
5	
6	
7	

Key term

tone a manner of expression in speech or writing

3   Professor Stephen Hawking's talk includes some big ideas. How effectively do you think he explains these for his audience? In your answer you should comment on:

■   the **tone** of the talk

■   the language he uses to present these ideas

■   the sequence of ideas and how the text is structured

■   any links you can find between ideas within and between paragraphs.

4   Read the following student's comment on the text:

Professor Hawking sounds so clever and this helps to convince you that what he's saying is right.

Do you agree or disagree with this statement? Refer to evidence from the text to support your view.

5   If you were asking Professor Stephen Hawking to give this same talk to an audience of primary school children, what changes would you advise him to make to appeal to this younger audience? Rewrite paragraph two as a guide.

Extended reading

Compare the extract from Richard Feynman's autobiography with the extract from the talk by Stephen Hawking in order to answer the following question.

Compare how the two writers convey their ideas in a way that helps the general reader to understand complex ideas. Use some or all of these questions to help structure your response.

- What form of non-fiction has been used by each writer and what effects do these create?

- How do the authors introduce their ideas and make the reader interested in them?

- Does each writer's use of language and sentence forms help to convey their ideas in a way the general reader can understand?

- How does the way each extract is structured contribute to the reader's understanding of the ideas presented?

Extended writing

Give a speech explaining what you think the greatest challenge faced by the human race is. In your speech you could draw on the ideas and techniques you have explored in Professor Stephen Hawking's talk.

As you write, think about:

- how you can begin your speech to hook the audience's interest and introduce the subject you will be talking about

- the tone you want to create and the language you can use to convey your ideas

- the structure of your speech and the way you can guide listeners to follow your ideas and arguments

- how the end of your speech could link back to the beginning and the final thought you want to leave your listeners with.

Remember to check the spelling, punctuation and grammar of your writing.

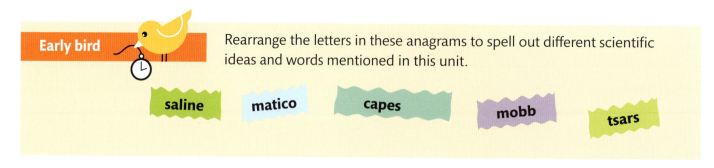

Early bird

Rearrange the letters in these anagrams to spell out different scientific ideas and words mentioned in this unit.

saline   matico   capes   mobb   tsars

Source texts table

Texts	Genre	Date
8.1 Grasmere journal by Dorothy Wordsworth	Journal	1802
8.2 'The summit of Scafell Pike' by Alfred Wainwright	Guide	1960
8.3 *The Old Ways* by Robert Macfarlane	Travel writing	2013

Big picture

From mountains, lakes and forests to ancient tracks and roads, different types of landscape have been an inspiration to writers through the ages. What is the most spectacular landscape that you have ever seen, in person or on screen?

In this section you will read three non-fiction texts that explore different aspects of the British landscape: an extract from the poet Dorothy Wordsworth's journals recording her life in the Lake District at the beginning of the 19th century; an extract from a walking guide written in the 20th century by Alfred Wainwright, describing the summit of Scafell Pike, the highest mountain in England; and an extract from *The Old Ways* by Robert Macfarlane, a book that describes the author's journey at the beginning of the 21st century following the ancient tracks that criss-cross the British Isles.

Skills

> **Key term**
>
> **setting** the place in which something is set

- Understand the meaning of a text
- Make inferences and refer to evidence in a text
- Comment on a writer's use of language and structure (including poetic language, mood, **setting**, paragraphing)
- Practise writing a journal entry, drawing on techniques and ideas explored in your reading

Before reading

1   Look at the following types of landscape.

forests and woods   moors   farmland   beaches   mountains

valleys   rivers and streams   hills   deserts   caves

Which of these types of landscape have you visited? Which would you say is the most appealing and which is the least? Give reasons for your choices.

2 Why do you think people enjoy visiting wild places? Discuss the following reasons and decide whether you agree or disagree with each one.

> Wild places provide an escape from the modern world.

> The beauty of wild places is inspirational.

> Wild places help connect us with the natural world.

> Wild places remind us why it's important to protect the landscape from development.

3 Copy the table below and make a list of arguments for and against holidaying in wild places. Think of the advantages and disadvantages for different types of visitors, for example, families with children, elderly people or adventurous adults.

Arguments for holidaying in wild places	Arguments against holidaying in wild places

8.1 Grasmere journal by Dorothy Wordsworth, 1802

The following extract is taken from a journal kept by Dorothy Wordsworth, the sister of the poet William Wordsworth, during her stay at Dove Cottage in Grasmere, a village in the Lake District in Cumbria. In the following entry written on Friday 16 April 1802, Dorothy Wordsworth describes a countryside walk with her brother. As you read, try to picture the scenes she describes.

Source text 8.1

WORD BANK

prospect a wide view

knolls small round hills; mounds

retiring avoiding company

sate archaic spelling of sat

turf short grass

pile wort a plant mostly found in hedgerows

Brothers Water a small lake

The Glow-worm a poem by William Wordsworth

When I undrew curtains in the morning, I was much affected by the beauty of the **prospect**, and the change. The sun shone, the wind had passed away, the hills looked cheerful, the river was very bright as it flowed into the lake. The church rises up behind a little knot of
5   rocks, the steeple not so high as an ordinary three-story house. Trees in a row in the garden under the wall. The valley is at first broken by little woody **knolls** that make **retiring** places, fairy valleys in the vale, the river winds along under these hills, travelling, not in a bustle but not slowly, to the lake. We saw a fisherman in the flat meadow on
10   the other side of the water. He came towards us, and threw his line over the two-arched bridge. It is a bridge of a heavy construction, almost bending inwards in the middle, but it is grey, and there is a look of ancientry in the architecture of it that pleased me. As we go on the vale opens out more into one vale, with somewhat of a cradle
15   bed. Cottages, with groups of trees, on the side of the hills. We passed a pair of twin children, two years old. **Sate** on the next bridge which we crossed a single arch. We rested again upon the **turf**, and looked at the same bridge. We observed arches in the water, occasioned by the large stones sending it down in two streams. A sheep came
20   plunging through the river, stumbled up the bank, and passed close to us. It had been frightened by an insignificant little dog on the other side. Its fleece dropped a glittering shower under its belly. Primroses by the road-side, **pile wort** that shone like stars of gold in the sun, violets, strawberries, retired and half-buried among the grass. When
25   we came to the foot of **Brothers Water**, I left William sitting on the bridge and went along the path on the right side of the lake through the wood. I was delighted with what I saw. The water under the boughs of the bare old trees, the simplicity of the mountains, and the exquisite beauty of the path. There was one grey cottage.
30   I repeated **The Glow-worm**, as I walked along. I hung over the gate, and thought I could have stayed for ever. When I returned, I found William writing a poem descriptive of the sights and sounds we saw and heard. There was the gentle flowing of the stream, the glittering,

WORD BANK

lasses girls or young women

wantonness unrestrained behaviour

Kirkstone a mountain pass

becks streams

Ambleside a town

the Luffs, the Roddingtons friends of the Wordsworth family

Rydale Lake a small lake

lively lake, green fields without a living creature to be seen on them;
behind us, a flat pasture with forty-two cattle feeding; to our left, the
road leading to the hamlet. No smoke there, the sun shone on the bare
roofs. The people were at work ploughing, harrowing, and sowing;
lasses spreading dung, a dog barking now and then, cocks crowing,
birds twittering, the snow in patches at the top of the highest hills,
yellow palms, purple and green twigs on the birches, ashes with their
glittering stems quite bare. The hawthorn a bright green, with black
stems under the oak. The moss of the oak glossy. We went on. Passed
two sisters at work (they first passed us), one with two pitchforks in
her hand, the other had a spade. We had come to talk with them.
They laughed long after we were gone, perhaps half in **wantonness**,
half boldness. William finished his poem. Before we got to the foot of
Kirkstone, there were hundreds of cattle in the vale. There we ate our
dinner. The walk up Kirkstone was very interesting. The **becks** among
the rocks were all alive. William showed me the little mossy streamlet
which he had before loved when he saw its bright green track in
the snow. The view above **Ambleside** very beautiful. There we sate
and looked down on the green vale. We watched the crows at a little
distance from us become white as silver as they flew in the sunshine,
and when they went still further, they looked like shapes of water
passing over the green fields. The whitening of Ambleside church is a
great deduction from the beauty of it, seen from this point. We called
at **the Luffs, the Roddingtons** there. Did not go in, and went round
by the fields. I pulled off my stockings, intending to wade the beck,
but I was obliged to put them on, and we climbed over the wall at the
bridge. The post passed us. No letters. **Rydale Lake** was in its own
evening brightness: the Island, and Points distinct. Jane Ashburner
came up to us when we were sitting upon the wall. We rode in her
cart to Tom Dawson's. All well. The garden looked pretty in the half-
moonlight, half-daylight, as we went up the vale of Brother's Water
more and more cattle feeding, 100 of them.

Basic reading skills

1 Look again at the first two sentences of the extract.

   a What does Dorothy Wordsworth say the weather is like in Grasmere on Friday 16 April 1802?

   b What do you think the weather has been like on the previous day? Pick out a quotation that suggests this.

2 Pick out the quotation that suggests that the first bridge that Dorothy Wordsworth crosses is an old bridge.

3 When Dorothy Wordsworth is resting on the grass and looking back at this bridge, what happens to make a sheep cross the river to the side where she is sitting?

4 William Wordsworth begins writing a poem while they are on their walk. What does Dorothy Wordsworth say this poem is about?

5a List three features of the landscape described by Dorothy Wordsworth that give you the impression this is a peaceful environment.

5b Pick out the quotation which you think gives this impression most effectively and explain your choice.

6a Create a map to show Dorothy and William Wordsworth's walk. You could refer to an actual map of the area around Grasmere to help you to mark the route of their journey.

6b Mark on your map the different sights that they saw, picking out relevant quotations from the text to help you to do this.

Advanced reading skills

Key term

sentence forms
sentence types (that is, statement, question, command, exclamation) and sentence structures (that is, simple, minor, multi-clause)

1 Dorothy Wordsworth describes passing two sisters who are working in the countryside and writes, 'They laughed long after we were gone, perhaps half in wantonness, half boldness.' Using your own ideas and words, explain why Dorothy Wordsworth thinks they were laughing.

2 This extract is taken from Dorothy Wordsworth's private journal. Note down three features that suggest this. You could think about:

- the details she includes

- her use of paragraphs

- her choice of **sentence forms**.

Key terms

prose writing or speech that is not in verse

noun phrase a group of words that has a noun as its key word

simile a comparison where one thing is compared to another using the words *like* or *as*

metaphor the use of a word or phrase which describes something by likening it to something else

3 Dorothy Wordsworth was a poet as well as a writer of **prose**.

a Look at the following extract from her journal entry and comment on how her use of language here is poetic:

'Its fleece dropped a glittering shower under its belly. Primroses by the road-side, pile wort that shone like stars of gold in the sun, violets, strawberries, retired and half-buried among the grass.'

b Pick out your own quotation that you think best suggests the poetic nature of Dorothy Wordsworth's language choices. Explain the effects that this quotation creates.

4 Read what this student says about the text:

Dorothy Wordsworth's writing conveys her love of the countryside.

a Copy the table below. Identify quotations which could support this student's statement. The first one has been done for you.

Quotation
'I was much affected by the beauty of the prospect'

b Choose one quotation from your table and explain how it conveys Dorothy Wordsworth's love of the countryside.

5 What impression do you get of Dorothy Wordsworth's feelings about the places she sees and passes on her walk? Explore how the following help to build this impression:

- her use of **noun phrases** to convey the scene
- her use of **similes** and **metaphors**
- the thoughts and feelings she shares in the journal entry.

8.2 'The summit of Scafell Pike' by Alfred Wainwright, 1960

Alfred Wainwright wrote a series of guides about the mountains of the Lake District in England during the 1950s and 1960s. In the following extract he describes the summit of Scafell Pike and reflects on why people enjoy walking in wild places. As you read, think about the writer's own attitude towards the Lake District fells.

Source text 8.2

WORD BANK

cairn a pile of stones set up as a landmark

edifice a building (usually large or grand)

triangulation column a concrete pillar originally set up for surveying purposes, usually noting the height of the land

Ordnance Survey Great Britain's national mapping agency

erring mistaken

promenade a paved public walkway for a leisurely stroll, often in a scenic place such as along a sea front

This is it: the place of many ceremonies and celebrations, of bonfires and birthday parties; the ultimate; the supreme; the one objective above all others; the highest ground in England; the top of Scafell Pike.

5 It is a magnet, not because of its beauty for this is not a place of beauty, not because of the exhilaration of the climb for there is no exhilaration in toiling upwards over endless stones, not because of its view for although this is good there are others better. It is a magnet simply because it is the highest ground in

10 England.

There is a huge **cairn** that from afar looks like a hotel; a well-built circular **edifice** now crumbling on its east side, with steps leading up to its flat top. Set into the vertical nine-foot north wall of the cairn is a tablet commemorating the gift of the summit to the

15 nation. A few yards distant, west, is a **triangulation column** of the **Ordnance Survey**; a visitor in doubt and seeking confirmation of his whereabouts should consult the number on the front plate of the column; if it is anything other than S.1537 he has good cause for doubt – heaven knows where his **erring** steps have led him, but

20 it is certainly not to the summit of Scafell Pike.

The surrounding area is barren, a tumbled wilderness of stones of all shapes and sizes, but it is not true, as has oft been written and may be thought, that the top is entirely devoid of vegetation: there is, indeed, a patch of grass on the south side of

25 the cairn sufficient to provide a couch for a few hundredweights of exhausted flesh.

Yet this rough and desolate summit is, after all, just as it should be, and none of us would really want it different. A smooth green **promenade** here would be wrong. This is the summit of England,

30 and it is fitting that it should be sturdy and rugged and strong.

Basic reading skills

1   Re-read the opening paragraph. Pick out three brief quotations that suggest the importance of Scafell Pike.

2   Now re-read the second paragraph. Why does the writer suggest Scafell Pike attracts so many visitors?

3   Which two of the following things can you find at Scafell Pike?

A hotel

An Ordnance Survey triangulation column

The magnetic pole

A patch of grass

4   Re-read the following quotation: 'The surrounding area is barren'.

Pick out two other quotations that give this impression.

Advanced reading skills

1a   Which of the following words do you think best describe the writer's feelings towards Scafell Pike?

embarrassed

amazed

proud

pitying

respectful

1b   Pick out a quotation that best suggests this feeling.

2   Re-read the opening paragraph. Comment on how the writer's use of sentence forms conveys an impression of the place he is writing about. You should comment on the effects created by:

- the multi-clause sentence

- the use of punctuation such as colons, semi-colons and commas.

3   Read what this student says about the description of Scafell Pike.

The writer makes it sound like a desolate place, devoid of any attractions.

Can you identify any quotations to support this statement? Explain your choices.

4   Now re-read the final paragraph. How does the impression the writer gives you of Scafell Pike change here?

5   What overall impression do you get of Scafell Pike from this extract? Think about:

- the **imagery** the writer chooses to describe the landscape

- how the writer reacts to the environment and the way these reactions are conveyed.

Key term

imagery writing which creates a picture or appeals to other senses; this includes simile, metaphor and personification and the use of vivid verbs, nouns, adjectives and adverbs

8.3 *The Old Ways* by Robert Macfarlane, 2013

The Old Ways is a non-fiction book by the travel and nature writer Robert Macfarlane which was first published in 2013. In this book he describes his journeys following the ancient tracks and routes that criss-cross the British Isles. In the following extract Robert Macfarlane describes a walk he takes from his house in Cambridge along the Icknield Way, an ancient track that stretches from Norfolk to Wiltshire. As you read, think about why Robert Macfarlane describes one of the first walks he undertook for the book.

Source text 8.3

WORD BANK

brocaded decorated with raised patterns (from the word 'brocade', a rich fabric woven with raised patterns)

briar a thorny bush

hawthorn a thorny tree with white or pink blossom and dark red berries

field maple a type of tree

dog-rose a type of flowering shrub

subsidiary secondary

Within a mile of my home in Cambridge runs the grassy Roman road I had followed on my winter night-walk. In spring its wide verges are **brocaded** with flowers, and for much of its length it is bordered by hedgerows of **briar**, **hawthorn** and **field maple**. Seven miles
5 south-east along it lies the village of Linton, through which passes the Icknield Way.

Just after dawn on a late May day I slipped out of the house while my family was asleep, got onto my bicycle and pedalled along quiet streets and paths – up onto the whaleback hill of chalk, past the great
10 open field behind the beech wood – before turning onto the Roman road. The forecast was for warm dry weather extending unbroken for a week to come. There were sixteen or seventeen hours of sunlight each day. The scent of **dog-rose** sweetened the air. A crow flopped from an ash tree, its wings silver with sun. I felt filled with a boyish excitement.
15 In my pack was a copy of Edward Thomas's *The Icknield Way*, his prose account of his journey along the Way.

I was cycling downhill along the Roman road, near the Iron Age ring-fort, when the accident happened. Happy to be on the move, I let the bicycle gather speed. The rutted path became rougher, my wheels
20 juddered and bounced, I hit a hunk of hard soil the size of a fist, the front wheel bucked and twisted through ninety degrees, the bike folded in upon itself and I crashed onto it, the end of the left handlebar driving hard into my chest. The breath was bashed out of me. There was a sharp grating pain in my ribcage. My elbow was bleeding and my
25 kneecap appeared to have grown a **subsidiary** purple kneecap. The severest injury appeared to be to my self-respect. What a fool I'd been, biking like a dizzy vicar down the road, too full of the romance of the way. I would have to limp home, not even two miles along my first path.

But after various diagnostic prods, it seemed that all might not
30 be lost. The kneecap was injured but unbroken. I had cracked a rib,

WORD BANK

metaphysics a branch of philosophy that deals with abstract concepts such as being, knowing, identity, time, and space

uroboros a circular symbol depicting a snake, or less commonly a dragon, swallowing its tail, as an emblem of wholeness or infinity

braid a plait of hair or a strip of cloth with a woven decorative pattern

caul the protective membrane that encloses a foetus

possibly two, but this seemed a minor impediment to walking. And the bicycle could, with some botched repairs, be just about persuaded to move. So I cycled on to Linton, slowly. A warning, I thought superstitiously, had been issued to me: that the going would not be easy,
35 and that romanticism would be quickly punished. It was only a few miles later that I remembered the letter a friend had sent me when I told him about my plan to walk the Icknield Way. Take care as you pass the ring-fort, he had written back. When I mentioned the fall later, he was unamazed. 'This was an entry fee to the old ways, charged at one of the
40 usual tollbooths,' he said. 'Now you can proceed. You're in. Bone for chalk: you've paid your due.' It was the first of several incidents along the old ways that I still find hard to explain away rationally.

Thomas followed the Icknield Way in 1911, in the depths of one of his worst depressions. He moved fast and then he wrote up the journey
45 fast, in a matter of weeks. *The Icknield Way* is an unconventional book: partly a guide to the history and geography of the Way, partly a meditation on its **metaphysics** and partly a record of Thomas's own bleak unhappiness. [...]

In the 1890s a folklorist called John Emslie had walked the Icknield
50 Way and collected the stories he heard told along the path. In many of these stories the Way – if followed far enough – passes out of the known and into the mythic, leading to kingdoms of great danger and reward. Emslie was told of one man who had 'travelled along this road till he came to the fiery mountains'. Another spoke of it as
55 going 'round the world, so that if you keep along it and travel on you will come back to the place you started from'. 'All along my route', wrote Emslie, he had heard similar tales: that the path 'went all round the world, or all through the island ... from sea to sea'. It was, in this respect, a path that stood as a prototype for all others, at last returning
60 **uroboros**-like to engulf its own origin.

Thomas was compelled by the Way's existence as a **braid** of stories and memories. In one of his most enigmatic prose passages he suggested that paths were imprinted with the 'dreams' of each traveller who had walked it, and that his own experiences would 'in
65 course of time [also] lie under men's feet'. [...]

In Linton, I hid my damaged bike behind a hedge and walked my damaged body out of the village by its main street, under a rising sun. The cloud **caul** was breaking up and a lemony light pushed through the gaps. The path led me past Linton Zoo and from
70 behind a high hedge came the grunts and calls of the inmates: zebras, lions, storks and cranes. I passed a thatched cottage with

hollyhocks bobbing in the wind at its walls, and roses by its doors. The visuals were deep England but the soundtrack was **Serengeti**.

75 Quickly I was onto the chalky field-edge footpaths whose route corresponded roughly to that of the Way. I went through a narrow tunnel of **spindle** and hawthorn. A brown hare belted along the track, halted, regarded me briefly, then pivoted on its hind legs and dashed back off and away, as if committed to the path's pursuit. Within an hour the sun was fully out. Skylarks pelted their song down, 80 lifting my spirit. Light pearled on barley. The shock of the crash began to fade away. Hawthorn hedges foamed white with flower and wood pigeons clattered from the ash canopies.

For the first eight miles of the day I saw no one at all, and had the peculiar feeling of occupying an evacuated landscape, post-apocalypse 85 or in civil lockdown. So few people now labour on the land that the people one tends to meet on footpaths are walkers, not workers.

I followed a continuous line of bare white chalk, moving by hedge and field-edge bearing roughly west-south-west. I met a covey of French partridges with their barred sides and Tintin-like 90 quiffs; three cock pheasants with their copper flank armour and white dog-collars (hoplite vicars); a grebe on a pond, punkishly tufted as **Ziggy Stardust**.

The landscape's emptiness spooked me, and it was an unexpected relief to hear the distant hum of the M11 motorway, growing to 95 a roar as I neared it. The motorway occupied exactly the place in the landscape that a river might have done, running where two chalk ranges dipped down into a valley, and the sun-strikes off windscreen and paintwork lent it the distant dazzle of moving water. I approached it on high ground through the sage green of young 100 cereal crops. Suddenly, above the roar of the cars, I heard someone singing. A ghostly high carolling, intermittent and tentative. It took a few seconds to understand that it was the song of the pylons, a long line of which marched away into the distance. I stood under one of them, listening to the spit and fizz of its energy, and the humming 105 note that formed, with the other pylons nearby, a loose chord.

Great Chesterford was the town where I **forded** the motorway. In houses near the road's edge, bird fanciers kept parakeets which hopped around in their cages on faded St George's flags, chirruping to one another. I rested on the motorway bridge, arms hung over the railings, 110 watching the rush of cars and the heat-waves rising from the asphalt. It was a perpendicular meeting of the Icknield Way (opened circa 4000 BC) and the M11 (opened 1975).

Basic reading skills

1 At what time of day does Robert Macfarlane begin the journey described in the extract?

2 Summarize the accident that Robert Macfarlane has on the early part of his journey. In your summary you should include:

- where the accident occurred
- what caused the accident
- the injuries that Robert Macfarlane suffered.

3 When Robert Macfarlane describes his accident to a friend, he is told: 'This was an entry fee to the old ways, charged at one of the usual tollbooths. Now you can proceed. You're in. Bone for chalk: you've paid your due.' Using your own words, explain what his friend means by this.

4 Robert Macfarlane is following in the footsteps of Edward Thomas, a poet and journalist who walked the Icknield Way in 1911. List two facts about Edward Thomas that you can find from the text.

5 List three different things that Robert Macfarlane hears on his journey.

6 Robert Macfarlane writes: 'The landscape's emptiness spooked me'.

a Pick out two quotations that you think best describe the emptiness of the landscape.

b Now re-read the final two paragraphs. Pick out three details that suggest he is leaving this emptiness behind.

Advanced reading skills

1 Choose one word from the list below that best describes the mood created by this extract.

lonely calm sinister bleak contemplative

Explain your choice of word.

2 Re-read the paragraph beginning, 'Quickly I was onto the chalky field-edge footpaths...'. How does the writer build a picture of the setting here? In your answer you should comment on:

- vocabulary choice
- the **verbs** and **adverbs** used
- the details chosen
- the choice of sentence forms.

3 In the text the writer describes his own experience of following the Icknield Way, but also writes about other people such as Edward Thomas and John Emslie who have walked this route.

a Re-read the text to identify the paragraphs where the writer focuses on the experiences and views of other people.

b Why do you think the writer has chosen to include these other views of the Icknield Way?

Key terms

verb a word that identifies actions, thoughts, feelings or the state of being

adverb a word that adds to the meaning of a verb, adjective or another adverb

4   Read what the following student says about the text:

> Robert Macfarlane describes the beauty of the natural world, but also conveys the beauty of the man-made environment too.

Do you agree with this statement? Copy and complete the table below by picking out quotations where the beauty of the natural world and the man-made environment is either explicitly shown or implied. Some examples have been given.

Natural world	Man-made environment
'The scent of dog-rose sweetened the air'	'the sun-strikes off windscreen and paintwork lent it the distant dazzle of moving water'

Extended reading

Choose two of the extracts you have read in this section and make notes about how each text creates a sense of place.

Now compare your two chosen extracts. In your comparison you should:

- identify the similarities and differences between the places described
- identify the techniques used to create a sense of each place
- explore how you respond to the places described as a reader
- evaluate which extract you think is the most successful in creating a sense of place and why.

Extended writing

Write a journal entry describing a journey that you have taken. This could be your journey to school or another journey you remember.

As you write, think about how you can draw on the techniques you explored in the extract from Dorothy Wordsworth's Grasmere journal as you create your own journal entry. You can also draw on different techniques from the other two texts you have read in this section.

Remember to check the spelling, punctuation and grammar of your writing.

Early bird

In the extract from *The Old Ways*, Robert Macfarlane writes, 'Great Chesterton was the town where I forded the motorway.' Rewrite this sentence using the following verbs in place of 'forded' and discuss the different effects these create.

traversed   **navigated**   **criss-crossed**   **cut across**

negotiated   **vaulted**   **passed over**   **bridged**

Poverty and homelessness

Source texts table

Texts	Genre	Date
9.1 *Down and Out in Paris and London* by George Orwell	Autobiography	1933
9.2 'A nightly scene in London' by Charles Dickens	Magazine article	1856
9.3 'The Foodbank Dilemma' by James Harrison	Magazine article	2014

Big picture

Throughout history people can be found living on the edge of despair, falling through the cracks in society because of poverty or homelessness. How do you think people become homeless or fall into poverty?

In this section you will read three non-fiction texts: an extract from *Down and Out in Paris and London*, an autobiography by George Orwell that describes his experiences of living as a tramp in London in 1928; a 19th-century magazine article written by Charles Dickens in which he describes an encounter with a homeless woman; and an extract from a 21st-century magazine exploring a rise in the number of people using foodbanks.

Skills

- Understand the meaning of a text

- Make inferences and refer to evidence in a text

- Comment on a writer's use of language (including vocabulary choices, sentence structures, **direct speech** and bias)

- Explore the techniques used by a writer to communicate views and ideas

- Practise writing a blog, drawing on techniques and ideas explored in your reading

Key term

direct speech when the words a person has spoken are relayed to the reader exactly, using speech marks

Before reading

1 What responsibility do you think we have as a society to people suffering from poverty or homelessness? Some people say that everyone should be able to support themselves but others argue that society should help those in difficulty. What do you think? Try to find evidence to support your point of view.

2 Read this comment and see if you agree with it: 'I always give money to homeless people as I imagine what it must be like to be in their shoes.'

Write a sentence explaining your opinion. Start the sentence with: 'I agree/disagree with the statement because...'

9.1 *Down and Out in Paris and London* by George Orwell, 1933

George Orwell was a writer and journalist whose novels include *Animal Farm* and *1984*. In 1928 he was living in London and decided to live as a tramp to explore the conditions for homeless people at this time. As you read, think about what impression you get of what life was like for a homeless person then.

Source text 9.1

WORD BANK

proprietor the owner of a shop or business

disparagingly in a belittling way

shilling a former British coin, equal to 5p

patina a film or sheen produced by age

To sell my clothes I went down into Lambeth, where the people are poor and there are a lot of rag shops. At the first shop I tried the **proprietor** was polite but unhelpful; at the second he was rude; at the third he was stone deaf, or pretended to be so. The fourth
5 shopman was a large blond young man, very pink all over, like a slice of ham. He looked at the clothes I was wearing and felt them **disparagingly** between thumb and finger.

'Poor stuff,' he said, 'very poor stuff, that is.' (It was quite a good suit.) 'What yer want for 'em?'
10 I explained that I wanted some older clothes and as much money as he could spare. He thought for a moment, then collected some dirty-looking rags and threw them on to the counter. 'What about the money?' I said, hoping for a pound. He pursed his lips, then produced A **SHILLING** and laid it beside the clothes. I did
15 not argue—I was going to argue, but as I opened my mouth he reached out as though to take up the shilling again; I saw that I was helpless. He let me change in a small room behind the shop.

The clothes were a coat, once dark brown, a pair of black dungaree trousers, a scarf and a cloth cap; I had kept my own shirt,
20 socks and boots, and I had a comb and razor in my pocket. It gives one a very strange feeling to be wearing such clothes. I had worn bad enough things before, but nothing at all like these; they were not merely dirty and shapeless, they had—how is one to express it?—a gracelessness, a **patina** of antique filth, quite different
25 from mere shabbiness. They were the sort of clothes you see on a bootlace seller, or a tramp. An hour later, in Lambeth, I saw a hang-dog man, obviously a tramp, coming towards me, and when I looked again it was myself, reflected in a shop window. The dirt was plastering my face already. Dirt is a great respecter of persons; it
30 lets you alone when you are well dressed, but as soon as your collar is gone it flies towards you from all directions.

WORD BANK

vagabond a person with no settled home or regular work

disparity difference

hawker someone who carries goods about to sell them

barrow a small cart that is pushed or pulled by hand

doss-house a cheap lodging house for homeless people

navvy an old-fashioned term for a labourer

etiolated pale and weak from lack of light

paregoric a type of medicine

I stayed in the streets till late at night, keeping on the move all the time. Dressed as I was, I was half afraid that the police might arrest me as a **vagabond**, and I dared not speak to anyone,
35 imagining that they must notice a **disparity** between my accent and my clothes. (Later I discovered that this never happened.) My new clothes had put me instantly into a new world. Everyone's demeanour seemed to have changed abruptly. I helped a **hawker** pick up a **barrow** that he had upset. 'Thanks, mate,' he said with
40 a grin. No one had called me mate before in my life—it was the clothes that had done it. For the first time I noticed, too, how the attitude of women varies with a man's clothes. When a badly dressed man passes them they shudder away from him with a quite frank movement of disgust, as though he were a dead cat. Clothes
45 are powerful things. Dressed in a tramp's clothes it is very difficult, at any rate for the first day, not to feel that you are genuinely degraded. You might feel the same shame, irrational but very real, your first night in prison.

At about eleven I began looking for a bed. I had read about
50 **doss-houses** (they are never called doss-houses, by the way), and I supposed that one could get a bed for fourpence or thereabouts. Seeing a man, a **navvy** or something of the kind, standing on the kerb in the Waterloo Road, I stopped and questioned him. I said that I was stony broke and wanted the cheapest bed I could get.

55 'Oh,' said he, 'you go to that 'ouse across the street there, with the sign "Good Beds for Single Men". That's a good kip [sleeping place], that is. I bin there myself on and off. You'll find it cheap AND clean.'

It was a tall, battered-looking house, with dim lights in all the
60 windows, some of which were patched with brown paper. I entered a stone passage-way, and a little **etiolated** boy with sleepy eyes appeared from a door leading to a cellar. Murmurous sounds came from the cellar, and a wave of hot air and cheese. The boy yawned and held out his hand.

65 'Want a kip? That'll be a 'og, guv'nor.'

I paid the shilling, and the boy led me up a rickety unlighted staircase to a bedroom. It had a sweetish reek of **paregoric** and foul linen; the windows seemed to be tight shut, and the air was almost suffocating at first. There was a candle burning, and I saw
70 that the room measured fifteen feet square by eight high, and had

queer strange

convex bulging outwards

counterpane a bedspread

eight beds in it. Already six lodgers were in bed, **queer** lumpy shapes with all their own clothes, even their boots, piled on top of them. Someone was coughing in a loathsome manner in one corner.

75 When I got into the bed I found that it was as hard as a board, and as for the pillow, it was a mere hard cylinder like a block of wood. It was rather worse than sleeping on a table, because the bed was not six feet long, and very narrow, and the mattress was **convex**, so that one had to hold on to avoid falling out. The

80 sheets stank so horribly of sweat that I could not bear them near my nose. Also, the bedclothes only consisted of the sheets and a cotton **counterpane**, so that though stuffy it was none too warm. Several noises recurred throughout the night. About once in an hour the man on my left—a sailor, I think—woke up, swore vilely,

85 and lighted a cigarette. Another man, victim of a bladder disease, got up and noisily used his chamber-pot half a dozen times during the night. The man in the corner had a coughing fit once in every twenty minutes, so regularly that one came to listen for it as one listens for the next yap when a dog is baying the moon. It was an

90 unspeakably repellent sound; a foul bubbling and retching, as though the man's bowels were being churned up within him. Once when he struck a match I saw that he was a very old man, with a grey, sunken face like that of a corpse, and he was wearing his trousers wrapped round his head as a nightcap, a thing which for

95 some reason disgusted me very much.

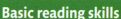

1 How many shops does the writer visit before he finds one where he is able to sell his clothes?

2 George Orwell writes, 'My new clothes had put me instantly into a new world.' Pick out two ways he says people treat him differently when wearing the dirty clothes the shopkeeper gave him.

3 Why does the writer say he dared not speak to anyone once he was wearing these new clothes?

4 Look again at the following extract from the text: 'Dressed in a tramp's clothes it is very difficult, at any rate for the first day, not to feel that you are genuinely degraded. You might feel the same shame, irrational but very real, your first night in prison.'

Rewrite the sentence in your own way to show what Orwell means. What does the extract suggest about the writer's feelings about his situation?

5 List four details about the room that the writer stays in overnight.

1 Re-read the first three paragraphs of the extract. How does the writer suggest the shopkeeper's attitude towards him? In your answer you should comment on:

- the shopkeeper's actions and the way these are described

- what the shopkeeper says

- how the writer responds to the shopkeeper.

2 Re-read the following sentence: 'I had worn bad enough things before, but nothing at all like these; they were not merely dirty and shapeless, they had—how is one to express it?—a gracelessness, a patina of antique filth, quite different from mere shabbiness.'

How effective is this sentence in giving you an impression of the writer's new clothes? In your answer you should comment on the effects created by:

- the contrast made with clothes the writer has worn before

- the vocabulary the writer chooses to describe the clothes

- the sentence structure and use of punctuation.

3 How does the writer's use of direct speech suggest how his situation has changed? Referring to the text, comment on what the direct speech suggests about the people the writer encounters.

4 Re-read the final paragraph beginning, 'When I got into the bed…'.

a Copy and complete the following table to identify how the writer uses different senses to describe his experience.

Touch	Smell	Hearing	Sight
'the bed… was as hard as a board'			

b Choose the sensory detail that you find most effective and explain how it helps you to imagine the writer's experience.

5 How does the writer's use of language help to give you an impression of how unpleasant he finds his situation throughout the extract? In your answer you should comment on:

- the writer's choices of vocabulary and descriptive details

- the **sentence forms** used and the effects these create.

Key term

sentence forms
sentence types (that is, statement, question, command, exclamation) and sentence structures (that is, simple, minor, multi-clause)

9.2 'A nightly scene in London' by Charles Dickens, 1856

Charles Dickens was a 19th-century writer and journalist whose novels, including *A Christmas Carol* and *Oliver Twist*, often explored the lives of the poor in Victorian Britain. Dickens was also the editor of a weekly magazine entitled *Household Words* in which the following article was first published on 26 January 1856. As you read, think about the impression the text gives you about how people in poverty lived at this time.

Source text 9.2

WORD BANK

Whitechapel a district in the East End of London

workhouse a public institution where people unable to support themselves were housed in return for work

Casual Ward the section of a workhouse where tramps and homeless people could stay for one night

On the fifth of last November, I, the Conductor of this journal, accompanied by a friend well-known to the public, accidentally strayed into **Whitechapel**. It was a
5   miserable evening; very dark, very muddy, and raining hard.

There are many woful sights in that part of London, and it has been well-known to me in most of its aspects for many years. We had forgotten the mud and rain in slowly walking along and
10 looking about us, when we found ourselves, at eight o'clock, before the **Workhouse**.

Crouched against the wall of the Workhouse, in the dark street, on the muddy pavement-stones, with the rain raining upon them, were five bundles of rags. They were motionless, and had no
15 resemblance to the human form. Five great beehives, covered with rags— five dead bodies taken out of graves, tied neck and heels, and covered with rags— would have looked like those five bundles upon which the rain rained down in the public street.

"What is this!" said my companion. "What is this!"
20 "Some miserable people shut out of the **Casual Ward**, I think," said I.

We had stopped before the five ragged mounds, and were quite rooted to the spot by their horrible appearance. Five awful Sphinxes by the wayside, crying to every passer-by, "Stop and guess! What is
25 to be the end of a state of society that leaves us here!"

As we stood looking at them, a decent working-man, having the appearance of a stone-mason, touched me on the shoulder.

"This is an awful sight, sir," said he, "in a Christian country!"

"GOD knows it is, my friend," said I.
30 "I have often seen it much worse than this, as I have been going home from my work. I have counted fifteen, twenty, five-and-twenty, many a time. It's a shocking thing to see."

WORD BANK

pauper a person who is very poor

porter a person whose job is to look after the entrance to a large building

disposition a person's nature or qualities

mollified calmed

"A shocking thing, indeed," said I and my companion together. The man lingered near us a little while, wished us good-night, and went on.

35 We should have felt it brutal in us who had a better chance of being heard than the working-man, to leave the thing as it was, so we knocked at the Workhouse Gate. I undertook to be spokesman. The moment the gate was opened by an old **pauper**, I went in, followed close by my companion. I lost no time in passing the old

40 **porter**, for I saw in his watery eye a **disposition** to shut us out.

"Be so good as to give that card to the master of the Workhouse, and say I shall be glad to speak to him for a moment."

We were in a kind of covered gateway, and the old porter went across it with the card. Before he had got to a door on our left, a man

45 in a cloak and hat bounced out of it very sharply, as if he were in the nightly habit of being bullied and of returning the compliment.

"Now, gentlemen," said he in a loud voice, "what do you want here?"

"First," said I, "will you do me the favor to look at that card in your hand. Perhaps you may know my name."

50 "Yes," says he, looking at it. "I know this name."

"Good. I only want to ask you a plain question in a civil manner, and there is not the least occasion for either of us to be angry. It would be very foolish in me to blame you, and I don't blame you. I may find fault with the system you administer, but pray understand that I know you

55 are here to do a duty pointed out to you, and that I have no doubt you do it. Now, I hope you won't object to tell me what I want to know."

"No," said he, quite **mollified**, and very reasonable, "not at all. What is it?"

"Do you know that there are five wretched creatures outside?"

60 "I haven't seen them, but I dare say there are."

"Do you doubt that there are?"

"No, not at all. There might be many more."

"Are they men? Or women?"

"Women, I suppose. Very likely one or two of them were there

65 last night, and the night before last."

"There all night, do you mean?"

"Very likely."

My companion and I looked at one another, and the master of the Workhouse added quickly, "Why, Lord bless my soul, what am

70 I to do? What can I do? The place is full. The place is always full—every night. I must give the preference to women with children, mustn't I? You wouldn't have me not do that?"

"Surely not," said I. "It is a very humane principle, and quite right; and I am glad to hear of it. Don't forget that I don't blame you."

75 "Well!" said he. And subdued himself again.

"What I want to ask you," I went on, "is whether you know anything against those five miserable beings outside?"

"Don't know anything about them," said he, with a wave of his arm.

80 "I ask, for this reason: that we mean to give them a trifle to get a lodging— if they are not shelterless because they are thieves for instance.—You don't know them to be thieves?"

"I don't know anything about them," he repeated emphatically.

"That is to say, they are shut out, solely because the Ward is full?"

85 "Because the Ward is full."

"And if they got in, they would only have a roof for the night and a bit of bread in the morning, I suppose?"

"That's all. You'll use your own **discretion** about what you give them. Only understand that I don't know anything about them

90 beyond what I have told you."

"Just so. I wanted to know no more. You have answered my question civilly and readily, and I am much obliged to you. I have nothing to say against you, but quite the contrary. Good night!"

"Good night, gentlemen!" And out we came again.

95 We went to the ragged bundle nearest to the Workhouse-door, and I touched it. No movement replying, I gently shook it. The rags began to be slowly stirred within, and by little and little a head was unshrouded. The head of a young woman of three or four and twenty, as I should judge; gaunt with want, and foul with dirt; but not naturally ugly.

100 "Tell us," said I, stooping down. "Why are you lying here?"

"Because I can't get into the Workhouse."

She spoke in a faint dull way, and had no curiosity or interest left. She looked dreamily at the black sky and the falling rain, but never looked at me or my companion.

105 "Were you here last night?"

"Yes. All last night. And the night afore too."

"Do you know any of these others?"

"I know her next but one. She was here last night, and she told me she come out of Essex. I don't know no more of her."

110 "You were here all last night, but you have not been here all day?"

"No. Not all day."

"Where have you been all day?"

"About the streets."

"What have you had to eat?"

115 "Nothing."

WORD BANK

shilling a former British coin, equal to 5p

lodging a room or rooms, not in a hotel, rented for living in

"Come!" said I. "Think a little. You are tired and have been asleep, and don't quite consider what you are saying to us. You have had something to eat today. Come! Think of it!"

"No I haven't. Nothing but such bits as I could pick up about the market. Why look at me!"

She bared her neck, and I covered it up again.

"If you had a **shilling** to get some supper and a **lodging**, should you know where to get it?"

"Yes. I could do that."

"For GOD's sake get it then!"

I put the money into her hand, and she feebly rose up and went away. She never thanked me, never looked at me—melted away into the miserable night, in the strangest manner I ever saw. I have seen many strange things, but not one that has left a deeper impression on my memory than the dull impassive way in which that worn-out heap of misery took that piece of money, and was lost.

Basic reading skills

1 Re-read the opening paragraph.

  a What part of London does Charles Dickens find himself in?

  b Pick out the quotation that suggests he didn't intend to visit this part of London.

2 Look again at the paragraph beginning, 'Crouched against the wall of the Workhouse…'. Using your own words, summarize what Charles Dickens sees outside the workhouse.

3a List three things Charles Dickens compares the figures he sees outside the workhouse to.

3b What impression do these comparisons give you of Dickens' feelings towards the figures? Give reasons for your answer.

4 Why does Charles Dickens decide to speak to the master of the workhouse? Choose the correct statement from the list below.

> **A.** He wants the master of the workhouse to take the women in.

> **B.** He wants to find out why the women haven't been allowed into the workhouse.

> **C.** He wants to impress the friend he is with.

> **D.** He wants to find out if the women outside the workhouse are thieves.

5 Why have the women been refused entry to the casual ward of the workhouse?

6 Which of the following groups of people does the master of the workhouse say are given preference?

A. The elderly   **C.** Children without parents

B. Women with children   **D.** Single women

7 Re-read the final paragraph.

a What does Charles Dickens do to help the woman?

b How does the woman respond to Dickens' help?

Advanced reading skills

1 Choose one word from the list below that best describes Dickens' feelings about the 'nightly scene' he describes in his article.

outraged   angry   disgusted   pleased   worried   shocked

Explain your choice of word.

2 Read what the following student says about the description of the figures Dickens sees outside the workhouse.

The way the figures are described makes it seem as if they aren't even human.

Can you identify any evidence to support this statement?

3 Charles Dickens tells the master of the workhouse: 'I don't blame you. I may find fault with the system you administer'. Find evidence from the text that suggests Dickens blames society for the situation he witnesses. Explain your choices.

4 Re-read the final section of the extract from the paragraph beginning, 'We went to the ragged bundle nearest to the Workhouse-door…'.

a Pick out one example of dialogue that you think best indicates the time the article was written. Explain your choice.

b What impression do you get of the homeless woman from this section? Think about:

- what she says and the way she says it

- her actions and the way these are described

- how Dickens responds to her.

c 'I have seen many strange things, but not one that has left a deeper impression on my memory than the dull impassive way in which that worn-out heap of misery took that piece of money, and was lost.' What does this sentence suggest about how the experience has affected Dickens?

9.3 'The Foodbank Dilemma' by James Harrison, 2014

A foodbank is a place where stocks of food are supplied free of charge to people in need. The following text is from an article that was first published in the *New Statesman* magazine on 21 October 2014. The author James Harrison describes his tour of a foodbank with the project manager of Coventry's foodbank network Hugh McNeil. As you read, think about the impression you get of the foodbank and the people who use it.

Source text 9.3

We leave the café and go down a narrow corridor, and arrive at a large storeroom. It's full of middle-aged women talking animatedly and sorting through provisions stacked on shelves from floor to ceiling. Tins of soup,

5 packets of pasta, cartons of juice. Too many different foodstuffs for me to make sense of it all. My eyes are drawn instead to the numbers scrawled in black highlighter pen everywhere.

"What are the numbers for?" I ask Hugh.

"Those are the use-by dates," he replies. "So we know when we

10 have to use the food. You don't want to give out food that is good until 2017, and then find that you have to throw away other tins and packets that have already gone off."

"Most of the food comes from collections from Tesco, Morrisons and Sainsbury's," Hugh tells me. "The supermarkets allow us to

15 give their customers a shopping list and we're then relying on the generosity of the people of Coventry to go in and buy a couple of extra items and give them to us. Just the annual collection we do at Tesco for three days every July should bring us in around ten tonnes of food from across the city."

20 "People do still donate at churches and other places. We literally have ten tonnes of beans. We have a 'bean room' at our central storehouse. People for some reason associate a foodbank with beans. But actually what we need is coffee, sugar, UHT milk, tinned fruit, tinned fish. A whole range of things. So we try and get the

25 shopping list to people and ask them to buy from it. But whatever you do, you still get lots of beans."

We leave the storeroom and go through a large hall at the back of the café, and out into a small back yard. A lorry is parked in the middle of the yard and younger men and women are sweating as

30 they heave down crates. They are jobseekers, getting some work experience as foodbank volunteers. The crates are full of fresh fruit and vegetables. Hugh says they've been donated by Costco.

WORD BANK

provisions supplies of food and drink

debt councillor a person whose job is to provide advice to people in financial difficulty

social housing accommodation that is affordable to people on low incomes

GP general practioners, also known as family doctors

When we get back to the café, there are people sitting at almost every table. I quickly scan the room: these are the people who have come to use the foodbank. Some are already sipping tea and coffee while they wait. At one table a volunteer is asking a couple if they have children. Then "Are you a vegetarian?" She ticks boxes on a form, and soon scuttles off to prepare three days' worth of **provisions**, tailored to the couple's needs.

There is a table set out by the entrance of the café, full of forms and papers. Tony, the volunteer co-ordinator, is greeting two new arrivals. A young clean-shaven man leads an older, grey-haired, battered-by-life-version-of-himself to where Tony stands. Tony greets them kindly and asks the younger man who referred them to the foodbank.

There's a moment of startled silence. Then the younger man says gruffly, "It's not for me, it's for my dad", and looks down at the floor. The colour flushing his face makes clear his embarrassment.

The older man appears confused until his son tells him to hand over the piece of paper he's holding in his hand. It transpires he's been sent to the foodbank by a **debt councillor** at Whitefriars, Coventry's largest provider of **social housing**. Tony takes a note of some numbers. All seems in order. He tells them to take a seat and someone will be over to see them shortly.

Hugh explains to me how the system works. "People are referred by specialist agencies from across the city," he says. "We work with over 250 agencies including churches, schools, housing agencies, **GP**'s surgeries and hospitals. Each person is entitled to 3 vouchers over a six month period. And each voucher entitles them to 3 days of food. We are there to help people with short-term crises. We aren't the long term solution to peoples' problems."

Hugh asks me if I want to meet some of the clients. I hesitate. More than anything else, this is what I have come for: to talk to people who use the foodbank, to understand why they have come and how they feel now that they are here. But suddenly I feel awkward and unsure, as if I'm pushing myself into the midst of a very private and sensitive process. At the same time, I see a journalist and photographer buzzing round the room talking to people and asking for pictures. I steel myself and agree to Hugh's offer.

He approaches a small, slight young woman, who is sitting crumpled and small on a chair in the corner. They talk. Even at a distance, I can tell that his infectious enthusiasm is beginning

←

75 to win her over. She slowly unfurls, brightening and then, a nod. Hugh beckons me over, introduces me; Louise is happy to have a chat.

"School holidays are the hardest time because you have to feed your children three times a day. That's why I am coming here now," she begins.

80 "The foodbank is wonderful. Normally I shop only from the value range and often I go round a couple of different supermarkets for the cheapest bargains so I can make my money stretch. And it's all tinned and frozen stuff – beans, pasta, that kind of thing. No fresh fruit or vegetables.

85 "Normally I eat porridge in the morning to fill myself up and then often I don't eat at all myself in the evenings. But today is the start of the kids' holidays and so they don't get the school meals, they have to eat all their food at home and I just can't manage, and so the foodbank is a lifeline."

90 Louise is a single mother with two young children. She has always found it a struggle to make ends meet, she says, and then she lost her **Employment Support Allowance** and **Disability Living Allowance** and was deemed fit for work. There is a garbled tale of an interview that went horribly wrong. She looks down at her feet.

95 She brightens again as she tells me about winning her appeal against the decision. But the appeal took six months and she's still waiting for the payout. In the meantime, she has struggled to feed and clothe her two children and pay all the bills. The school holidays and the extra financial pressure they bring were the final
100 straw. That's what brought her here today.

At one point the journalist, from the *Independent*, comes over to see if I'm finished. She sits for a while, notepad poised. But she realises that we have wandered off foodbanks and onto our very different experiences of parenthood, and she drifts off again. Louise
105 grows in confidence as she tells her story. I wonder if, as a single mother, Louise ever talks about her problems to anyone other than Jobcentre staff, lawyers and healthcare professionals.

"The foodbank is great because there are a couple of nice puddings and a pizza in there, some cornflakes and chocolate
110 biscuits. Stuff I would never normally be able to buy. The only other way to get something nice like that is to talk to the local shoplifter who can get you a nice piece of meat at a price you can

WORD BANK

Employment Support Allowance a benefit paid to people who are unable to work due to illness or disability

Disability Living Allowance a benefit paid to support people who have a disability

→

115 afford. People do use him, but you can't really blame them. Like my neighbours. They've been to the foodbank too. They both work. But they never know how much work they're going to get, and sometimes it's just not enough. It's horrible not being sure you can put food on the table for your family."

And then a smiling foodbank volunteer comes over, weighed down with shopping bags. Louise's eyes light up as the woman puts 120 the bags down in front of her. They sag outwards to display their contents. I see Louise catch sight of the bright shiny wrapping paper of two Easter Eggs perched on a solid base of soup, beans and pasta. She blinks back the tears. For a moment I think she will break down and fall into the volunteer's arms. But she settles for a 125 series of heartfelt 'thank yous'. The volunteer smiles again, a real joyful bottom-of-the-heart-smile this time.

Louise thanks me for the chat. We awkwardly wish each other well for the future. And she is off, out of the bright glass doors of the café and up the street. I am left thinking about Louise's story, 130 the story of her neighbours, and the feeling of joy we all felt when her food arrived.

Basic reading skills

1   In the storeroom the writer says he sees 'numbers scrawled in black highlighter pen everywhere'. What information do these numbers give?

2a List the names of three supermarkets who collect food for the foodbank.

2b Name one other type of place where people donate food to the foodbank.

3   The writer describes two men, one young and one old, waiting to use the foodbank. When asked who referred them to the foodbank, 'the younger man says gruffly, "It's not for me, it's for my dad."' What does this suggest about how the younger man feels about using the foodbank?

4   Which of the following statements best describes the role of the foodbank?

   A. To help people with short-term crises.

   B. To provide a long-term solution to people's problems.

   C. To help families during the school holidays.

   D. To provide people with luxury food items.

5 Re-read the paragraph beginning, 'Hugh asks me if I want to meet some of the clients.'

    a Using your own words, explain why the writer isn't sure about meeting some of the people who use the foodbank.

    b What convinces the writer to meet some of the clients?

    c Look again at the sentence, 'I steel myself and agree to Hugh's offer.' What does the word 'steel' mean in this context?

6 Give three factors that have led Louise to use the foodbank.

7 Select a quotation that you think best suggests Louise's gratitude towards the foodbank. Explain your choice of quotation.

Advanced reading skills

1 What do you think the writer's view of foodbanks is? Support your opinion with reference to the text.

2 Look at the following student's statement:

People only use foodbanks to get free food, not because they can't afford to eat.

    a Find three pieces of evidence from the text to challenge this point of view.

    b Look at the pieces of evidence you have identified and select the one that you think would be the most effective in changing this student's mind. Give reasons for your choice.

3 How does the way the writer uses language to describe the users of the foodbank influence your responses as a reader to them? Explore the use of language in the following sentences:

'A young clean-shaven man leads an older, grey-haired, battered-by-life-version-of-himself to where Tony stands.'

'He approaches a small, slight young woman, who is sitting crumpled and small on a chair in the corner.'

In your answer you should comment on:

- the writer's use of **noun phrases** and the effects these create
- the writer's choice of **verbs** and **adjectives** and the impression these give
- the sentence forms and the effects these create.

4 Look at the following statement from a student about this text:

This article is **biased** and only provides a one-sided view of foodbanks.

Do you agree or disagree with this statement? Find evidence from the text to support your point of view.

Key terms

noun phrase a group of words that has a noun as its key word

verb a word that identifies actions, thoughts, feelings or the state of being

adjective a word that describes a noun

biased a biased opinion is one based on one viewpoint which doesn't examine the facts fairly

Extended reading

Revisit two of the extracts you have read in this section in order to answer the following question.

Compare how the two writers use language to influence the reader's point of view. In your answer you should:

- identify the topic each writer is writing about
- compare the language choices each writer makes
- explore how each writer attempts to influence the reader's point of view through these language choices
- support your ideas with references to both texts.

Extended writing

'In over 150 years nothing has really changed in the way society looks after the poor.'

Write a blog in response to this statement. In the blog you should present your own point of view and can draw on evidence from the texts you have read in this section. As you write, think about:

- how you can introduce your opinion on this subject
- how you can structure your blog to develop the points you make
- how you can use language to influence readers to agree with your opinion
- how you can end your blog in an effective way.

Remember to check the spelling, punctuation and grammar of your writing.

Early bird

A synonym is a word that means the same or almost the same as another word. One synonym for the term 'opinion' is 'point of view'. How many more synonyms can you suggest for this term?

Why Shakespeare?

Source texts table

Texts	Genre	Date
10.1 'Why I hate Shakespeare' by Krystie Lee Yandoli	Blog	2014
10.2 *William Shakespeare's Romeo and Juliet* review by Peter Travers	Review	1996
10.3 *Richard II* with Mr Kean (Anonymous)	Review	1825

Big picture

William Shakespeare is celebrated by many as the greatest writer who ever lived. How much do you know about him and his plays?

Some people feel that we spend too much time studying Shakespeare and that his plays are no longer relevant for the world we live in today. In this section, you will read three non-fiction texts that present different views of Shakespeare and his work: a blog by Krystie Lee Yandoli about why she hates Shakespeare; a review of the 1996 film *William Shakespeare's Romeo and Juliet* from *Rolling Stone* magazine; and a review of a performance of *Richard II* in 1825.

Skills

- Understand the meaning of a text
- Make inferences and refer to evidence in a text
- Comment on a writer's use of language and structure (including chronological presentation, **metaphor**, **adjectives** and **sentence forms**)
- Explore the techniques used by a writer to communicate views and ideas
- Practise writing a review, drawing on techniques and ideas explored in your reading

Before reading

Key terms

metaphor the use of a word or phrase which describes something by likening it to something else

adjective a word that describes a noun

sentence forms sentence types (that is, statement, question, command, exclamation) and sentence structures (that is, simple, minor, multi-clause)

1   Discuss when and how you have encountered Shakespeare's work in school and how you have felt about this. Think about:

- your experiences of Shakespeare at primary and secondary school
- what you have enjoyed and disliked about studying Shakespeare.

2   How do you think the teaching of Shakespeare in schools could be improved? Consider some of the following suggestions:

> We should translate his plays into modern-day English to make them easier to understand.

> We should learn more about Shakespeare's life and times to understand his plays better.

> We should watch the plays in performance, not study them on the page.

> We should just focus on the exciting bits of each play and not have to read the whole thing.

If you had the chance to give your own view about how Shakespeare should be taught in your school, what recommendations would you make?

10.1 'Why I hate Shakespeare' by Krystie Lee Yandoli, 2014

The following blog was published on 10 April 2014 on BuzzFeed, a US news and entertainment website, in the run-up to the 450th anniversary of Shakespeare's birth. Here, Krystie Lee Yandoli, an American editor and writer, explains why she hates Shakespeare. As you read the text, think about whether you agree or disagree with the reasons she gives.

Source text 10.1

The literary world is gearing up to celebrate Shakespeare's 450th birthday this month. But I won't be participating. [...]

One May afternoon I sat in my high school's library with a small audience of my peers to see what work of literature I'd go home with.
5 I nearly jumped up when my name was called and hastily walked to the front of the group, but my heart sunk when the American Association of University Women handed me a copy of *The Complete Works of William Shakespeare*. I hate William Shakespeare.

As an avid reader and writer, I've been encouraged to read and love
10 Shakespeare throughout my life. I grew up familiar with the story of *Romeo and Juliet* and was surrounded by popular Shakespeare adaptations like *West Side Story* and *10 Things I Hate About You*, but the first time I had to actually read Shakespeare was in my sixth-grade language arts class. Our teacher read a number of acts
15 from *Hamlet* out loud in class, and then we were assigned to finish the rest of the play at home.

My teacher took the time to go over everything line by line when we read it in class, but when I took *Hamlet* home and it was just me, myself, and Shakespeare, I was beyond lost. I sifted through the
20 yellow, plastic hardcover book that creaked with each turn of the page, and all I learned was that Early Modern English hurt my brain and I couldn't seem to wrap my head around it. [...]

A handful of students raised their hands to excitedly give their two cents about the characters, themes, and dialogue in *Hamlet*. The
25 rest of the class remained as quiet as I did, but I didn't think I could necessarily take their silence for solidarity. After all, I had been told time and again that Shakespeare is "the greatest writer of all time."

For a while, Shakespeare was difficult for me to make sense of and understand. As time went on I became more capable of
30 comprehending what was going on in his plays, but I didn't grow to enjoy them any more. In high school I got around to reading *The Taming of the Shrew*, which I found problematic and, in turn,

MR. WILLIAM
SHAKESPEAR'S
COMEDIES,
HISTORIES, &
TRAGEDIES
1685

Methuen and Co., London

unenjoyable. From the way Katherine's character is portrayed as harsh and bitchy because she doesn't want to get married —
35 meanwhile, her younger sister Bianca who happens to be more docile is therefore more appealing to male suitors — to the plot revolving around how Katherine needs to be "tamed" until she turns into an obedient and subservient wife in a marriage she's forced into, all the way down to the play's title itself, *The Taming of the Shrew* did nothing
40 but irritate my budding feminist identity.

Sure, it's reflective of the time period it was written in — racial, gender, and sexual equality hadn't yet reached 16th century England — but that doesn't make me any more inclined to relish in what I interpret to be Shakespeare's inherent sexism. If I don't like
45 reading modern stories and authors that perpetuate sexist ideals about gender, love, and marriage, why should I make an exception for Shakespeare? Instead of devoting all of this literary space and obsessing over the words written by an author who celebrates his 450th birthday this month, I could be focusing on other important
50 writers from both past and present who offer different and equally important perspectives.

The dominant narrative is, more often than not, determined by society's elite. I'd rather not put an old, rich, white man from regal Britain and his **antiquated ideologies** about society on a pedestal.
55 In part, he's as influential and significant as he is because of the other old white men in power who decided he would be, and who made those decisions as to which literature gets **canonized**.

Throughout my entire academic career and even in professional circles, I couldn't help but feel insecure about my lack of enthusiasm
60 for Shakespeare, because for the vast majority of the time, I felt alone in my reluctance toward the author. From grade school through higher education, we're all taught to admire **the Bard**, and there's great shame attached to saying you don't like this literary icon.

Every time someone brings up *Macbeth* or *The Tempest*, I feel
65 like I have a knot in my stomach because all I ever wanted in the world is to be taken seriously as a writer and lover of literature, and I never thought that could happen if I admitted to my disdain for Shakespeare.

I've carried this secret insecurity around with me for as long as I've
70 been reading Shakespeare because I fear the judgment and ridicule of others, but why should I have to force myself to read something that's

supposed to be enjoyable? Despite the long road to get here, I've come to terms with my unpopular opinion. I no longer fear the judgment of others, and I unapologetically proclaim that, to me, Shakespeare is
75 highly overrated.

It's been seven years since I received my book award as a junior in high school, and I still have the copy of *The Complete Works of William Shakespeare* that the American Association of University Women gave me. It's a beautiful book covered in red velvet cloth-like material, the
80 pages lined in gold coloring. Its physical nature is absolutely gorgeous and I'll probably have it forever, but unfortunately all it'll ever do is look pretty and collect dust on my bookshelf.

Basic reading skills

1a Re-read the first paragraph. Which book does the writer say she was given at school?

1b Now re-read the final paragraph. Why was the writer given this book?

2 Name two adaptations of the Shakespeare play *Romeo and Juliet* that the writer says she was aware of when she was growing up.

3a Identify the name of the first Shakespeare play that the writer studied at school.

Romeo and Juliet   **The Tempest**   **The Taming of the Shrew**   **Hamlet**   **Macbeth**

3b Which of the following reasons does the writer give to explain why she found studying this text difficult?

> **A.** She found it difficult to understand the language the play was written in.

> **B.** She had to read it aloud in class.

> **C.** She thought the play was sexist.

> **D.** She was told Shakespeare is 'the greatest writer of all time'.

Pick out the quotation that best supports the reason you have chosen.

4 'I'd rather not put an old, rich, white man from regal Britain and his antiquated ideologies about society on a pedestal.' Explain what this statement means using your own words.

5 The writer says, 'I couldn't help but feel insecure about my lack of enthusiasm for Shakespeare.' Pick out two quotations from the text which suggest the writer's insecurity.

Advanced reading skills

1 Create a timeline showing the writer's encounters with the work of William Shakespeare. On your timeline you should identify:

- specific plays the writer is aware of or has studied
- when she encountered these plays
- any feelings she shares about these.

2 Look at the following student's comment about the structure of this blog:

The way the writer organizes the blog chronologically, taking the reader through her experiences of Shakespeare through school and into her academic career, is very effective. I think this helps to convince the reader to agree with her view of Shakespeare as the evidence to support why she doesn't like him is built up over time.

Do you agree or disagree with this student's comment? Refer to the text to support your point of view.

3 The writer states, 'I've been encouraged to read and love Shakespeare throughout my life.' Pick out two quotations that show the writer being encouraged to read and love Shakespeare.

4 Look at the following quotations and explain how the vocabulary the writer uses to describe Shakespeare helps to convey her negative opinion of him.

- 'Shakespeare's inherent sexism'
- 'an old, rich, white man from regal Britain and his antiquated ideologies'

5 Re-read the final three paragraphs of the text. How does the writer convey how her feelings about Shakespeare have changed? In your answer you should comment on:

- the use of metaphor to suggest her feelings
- the writer's choices of vocabulary and descriptive details
- the sentence forms used and the effects these create.

10.2 *William Shakespeare's Romeo and Juliet* review by Peter Travers, 1996

In 1996 the director Baz Luhrmann released *William Shakespeare's Romeo and Juliet*, his film adaptation of Shakespeare's play. The following text is an extract from a review of this film which was first published in *Rolling Stone* magazine on 1 November 1996. As you read the review, decide what the reviewer's opinion of the film is.

Source text 10.2

WORD BANK

dis disrespect

fervor American spelling of *fervour*; intense and passionate feeling

audacious bold or daring

Quentin Tarantino a film director known for the violent action in his films

Southern belle a wealthy, privileged woman from the southern states of the USA

volatile unpredictable and unstable

rabid flamboyance extreme showiness

Gen X Generation X, the generation born between 1960 and 1980, typically perceived to be disaffected and directionless

Leonardo DiCaprio is 21, Claire Danes is 17 [...] in *William Shakespeare's Romeo and Juliet.* You almost laugh watching them put a hip, hotblooded spin on the Bard's star-crossed lovers. No **dis** intended. The laughter comes from delight and awe at how well
5 DiCaprio and Danes pull off the trick. These babes from the TV woods — he started in *Growing Pains;* she emerged in *My So-Called Life* — fill their classic roles with vital passion, speak the Elizabethan verse with unforced grace, find the spirited comedy of the play without losing its tragic **fervor** and keep their balance when the **audacious** Australian
10 director Baz Luhrmann hurls them into a whirlwind of hardball action, rowdy humor and rapturous romance.

It's a good thing that Shakespeare gets his name in the title, or you might mistake the opening scenes for **Quentin Tarantino's** *Romeo and Juliet.* No dialogue, just gunshots, as two gang families — the
15 Montagues and the Capulets (each has its name in lights on the roof of a high-rise) — go to war. Welcome to mythical Verona Beach, where the gangs fire on each other, and soldiers in choppers fire on them. [...]

Juliet's papa Capulet is robustly played by Paul Sorvino [...]. Her
20 mother, Gloria (Diane Venora), is a **Southern belle** out to marry off her daughter to Paris (Paul Rudd), a wealthy square who comes dressed as an astronaut to a costume ball. Juliet's bawdy nurse is played by the British actress Miriam Margolyes with a broad Hispanic accent (she calls her mistress Wholiette). The excellent
25 John Leguizamo is Juliet's cousin Tybalt, a **volatile** Latino who's in a gang that likes to dude up and then accessorize with pearl-handle guns and silver boot heels. Romeo's clan is led by Dad (Brian Dennehy) and Mom (Christina Pickles) Montague. Their gang favors shorts and Hawaiian shirts. [...]
30 If your head isn't spinning yet, it will. The **rabid flamboyance** of Luhrmann's vision, remarkably accented by Kym Barrett's costumes and Catherine Martin's production design, is meant to make *Romeo and Juliet* accessible to the elusive **Gen X** audience without leaving the play

bowdlerized and broken. Luhrmann, known as a wizard in his native
35 **Oz**, where he stages plays and operas, relishes knocking cobwebs off classics.

Of course, messing with *Romeo and Juliet* is nothing new. It's been made over as a ballet, as a Broadway musical and Oscarwinning movie (*West Side Story*), and as a 1987 Abel Ferrara gang film (*China
40 Girl*). But all those productions threw out Shakespeare's language. Luhrmann and his Aussie co-writer, Craig Pearce, stick with the Bard's funny way of talking. **Iambic pentameter** in this **pulp context** may throw you at first, but hang on.

Director Franco Zeffirelli stuck to the language and the period in
45 his 1968 film *Romeo and Juliet* but livened things up by casting young leads — Olivia Hussey, 15, and Leonard Whiting, 17 [...] The film was a smash, though Zeffirelli cut the text severely to make up for the inadequacies of his otherwise-appealing actors.

Luhrmann cuts the text as well, though not as damagingly. His
50 point is not to distract you from the words, as Zeffirelli did, but to lead you to them. And in DiCaprio and Danes, who give magnetic performances, he has found two actors with the youth to play the roles and the talent to do them justice. They speak the verse so naturally that the meaning registers.

55 DiCaprio is dynamite in a role that builds on [his] rare talent [...]. As Romeo, he doesn't round his vowels (*tonight* becomes *tanight*) or **enunciate** in **dulcet** tones, but when he speaks, you believe him. Whether Romeo is lovesick ("Did my heart love till now?"), violent ("Tempt not a desperate man") or drugged ("A dateless bargain to
60 engrossing death"), DiCaprio lets the Bard's words flow with an ardor that you can't buy in acting class.

Danes, with poise beyond her years [...] is DiCaprio's equal. Juliet can be played as a ninny, a role Danes has been saddled with in other films [...]. She wisely chooses to emphasize Juliet's melting loveliness
65 and bristling wit. [...]

For all the tumult that Luhrmann stirs up in the film, he shoots the scenes between the two lovers with elegant simplicity. When Romeo first sees Juliet at the costume ball, his "bright angel" is wearing wings. He is dressed in a knight's shining armor. These children of
70 enemies steal looks at each other on opposite sides of a fish tank and later steal a kiss. [...]

Without the right actors, puppy love could never become the grand passion that tragedy requires after Romeo and Juliet are secretly married by Father Laurence (a splendid Pete Postlethwaite)
75 in defiance of their families. DiCaprio delivers the line "I am fortune's fool" with wrenching power as violence seals his fate. Luhrmann goes hog wild for the climactic double suicide on a flower-strewn altar lit by 2,000 candles, with Romeo swallowing a lethal drug picked up from a seedy dealer and Juliet holding a semiautomatic to her head.
80 Amid the clamor from outraged purists and Shakespeare spinning in his Stratford-on-Avon, England, grave, you should notice that Luhrmann and his two bright angels have shaken up a 400-year-old play without losing its touching, poetic innocence.

Basic reading skills

1 Using the information from the text, create a cast list for *William Shakespeare's Romeo and Juliet*. In the cast list you should include the name of the character and the actor who played them. The first part has been done for you.

   Romeo Leonardo DiCaprio

2 Why does the writer suggest a viewer might almost laugh watching Leonardo DiCaprio and Claire Danes play the parts of Romeo and Juliet? Pick out a quotation to support your answer.

3 Look again at the second paragraph. Why might the film be called *Quentin Tarantino's Romeo and Juliet* by mistake? How is this mistake avoided?

4 Other film adaptations of *Romeo and Juliet* mentioned by the writer include *West Side Story* and *China Girl*. What does the writer say is the key difference between these adaptations and Baz Luhrmann's film?

5a Copy and complete the following sentence to summarize the writer's feelings about this film.

   I think the reviewer feels the film is...

5b Pick out one quotation from the text that you think best illustrates the writer's feelings. Explain your choice of quotation.

1 The adjectives the writer chooses to describe the film he is reviewing can influence a reader's opinion. What impression do the adjectives used in the following quotation give you: 'hip, hotblooded spin on the Bard's star-crossed lovers'?

2 The two lead actors in *William Shakespeare's Romeo and Juliet* are Leonardo DiCaprio and Claire Danes.

    a Copy and complete the table below by picking out quotations where the writer conveys his view about their performances.

Leonardo DiCaprio	Claire Danes

    b Choose one quotation from each column of the table and explore how it conveys the writer's view about the selected actor's performance.

3 What impression do you get of the writer's opinion of this film? Explore how the following help to build this impression:

- the way the acting is described

- the way the directing is described

- the way the writer presents his own thoughts and feelings about the film.

4 Look at the following statement about what a film review should do: 'A good review should help you decide whether it is worth spending money to see a film.'

Explain whether you think this text is a good review. Refer to evidence from the text to support your answer.

10.3 *Richard II* with Mr Kean, 1825

The following text is a review of a performance of William Shakespeare's play *Richard II* at the Theatre Royal in London which was first published in *The Guardian* newspaper on 3 September 1825. The play starred Edmund Kean, a famous Shakespearean actor of the time, in the title role. As you read the review, think about the impression the reviewer gives you of Edmund Kean's performance.

Source text 10.3

WORD BANK

irresolute uncertain

monotonous declamation dull and tedious speech because there is no variation in tone or volume

farce comedy with exaggerated humour

On Saturday night last, Shakspeare's play of Richard II was performed, the part of Richard by Mr. Kean, previous to his departure for America. The character is heavy in representation, and requires talent of the very highest order to prevent its being felt
5 tedious by the audience: and it is therefore no slight compliment to the talents of Mr. Kean to say that he kept alive the interest of the piece to the last.

The **irresolute** changeable monarch was exhibited with great force and truth, while the reflecting and moralizing parts, which,
10 from the lips of an inferior performer, would have been scarcely endurable, were, by Mr. Kean's varied and pointed delivery, made the most interesting part of the performance. After being accustomed to listen to the **monotonous declamation** so common in our theatres, where every succeeding sentence is, with
15 the view of making it tell, given the same degree of effort as that which preceded it, and consequently where nothing tells forcibly, it is a high treat to hear the fine language of Shakespeare from the mouth of Kean.

In the after-piece of Of Age To-Morrow, the part of Frederick
20 Baron Willinghurst was undertaken by Mr. Kean, and in it he certainly displayed sufficient versatility. He sang, danced, and even tumbled, being apparently inclined to amuse himself as well as the audience. The dignity of the great tragedian was put aside for the broadest **farce** – an experiment of the policy of which we cannot
25 help doubting.

The house was tolerably well filled, but not crowded; and there were only about 20 ladies in the lower boxes. After the falling of the curtain, there was a loud and pretty general cry for Mr. Kean, to which, for a long time, he appeared to pay no attention. The call,
30 however, continued without intermission for about a quarter of an hour, at the end of which time he made his appearance. [...]

WORD BANK

oratorial to do with speech

obscuration lack of clearness, difficulty

Though a very good actor, Mr. Kean is, in his soberest moments, a very indifferent speech-maker, and on this occasion his **oratorial** powers evidently laboured under considerable **obscuration**.
35 However he "did address himself to speech," and uttered a pretty considerable quantity of nonsense which we shall not trouble ourselves with repeating.

Basic reading skills

1 Re-read the first paragraph. Pick out the quotation that suggests that the character of Richard II is a difficult part for an actor to play.

2 Look again at the second paragraph. List three features of Edmund Kean's performance that the reviewer praises.

3 Re-read the third paragraph which describes the performance of the after-piece *Of Age To-Morrow* in which Edmund Kean plays the part of Frederick Baron Willinghurst.

   a Pick out three differences between Edmund Kean's performance as Richard II and his performance as Frederick Baron Willinghurst.

   b The reviewer writes: 'The dignity of the great tragedian was put aside for the broadest farce – an experiment of the policy of which we cannot help doubting.' Using your own words, explain what the reviewer thinks about Edmund Kean's performance in the after-piece.

4 Pick out a quotation that suggests the audience enjoyed Edmund Kean's performance.

5 Re-read the final paragraph and summarize what happened when Edmund Kean returned to the stage.

Advanced reading skills

1 Look again at the opening paragraph of the review. How does this try to hook the reader's interest?

2 Re-read the second paragraph. How does the writer's choice of sentence structure and punctuation here help to convey his opinion of the performance? You should comment on:

   ■ the use of main and subordinate clauses and the information these give

   ■ the effects created by the use of commas

   ■ the length of the sentence and the effect this creates.

3 Re-read the second paragraph beginning 'The irresolute changeable monarch…'. Comment on the impression the writer's use of verbs and adjectives give you of his opinion towards Edmund Kean's performance. You should refer to at least one of the following quotations and find your own example from the text.

- ◼ 'The irresolute changeable monarch was exhibited with great force and truth'

- ◼ 'Mr. Kean's varied and pointed delivery'

- ◼ 'it is a high treat to hear the fine language of Shakespeare from the mouth of Kean'

4 Look again at the final paragraph. How does the writer's use of language and sentence forms help to convey how his opinion of Edmund Kean's performance has changed? In your answer you should comment on:

- ◼ the **tone** of the writing

- ◼ his vocabulary choices and the effects these create

- ◼ how other language features and sentence forms contribute to give you an impression of his opinion.

> **Key term**
>
> **tone** a manner of expression in speech or writing

Extended reading

Compare the two reviews you have read in this section, the *Rolling Stone* review of *William Shakespeare's Romeo and Juliet* and *The Guardian* review of *Richard II* in order to answer the following question:

Compare how the two writers use language to convey their opinion of the film or play they are reviewing. In your answer you should:

- identify the writer's opinions in both texts
- compare the language choices each writer makes
- explore how these language choices help to convey their opinions
- explain which you think is the most effective review
- support your ideas with references to both texts.

Extended writing

Write a review of a book you have read, a film, play or TV show you have watched or a video game you have played. This review will be published in the 'Entertainment' section of your school magazine. In your review you should:

- give a brief **synopsis** of the film, play, video game or TV show you are reviewing
- give your opinion on different aspects, such as the acting in a film, play or TV show, or the graphics in a video game
- give a recommendation on whether it is worth reading, watching or playing.

Remember to check the spelling, punctuation and grammar of your writing.

Key term

synopsis summary

Early bird

Some reviews use a star rating. For each star rating below, suggest three comments you might expect to find in a review of a film with this star rating. One been started for you.

1 star – This film is a total turkey. A cinematic disaster.

2 stars –

3 stars –

4 stars –

5 stars –

EXPERIENCE

RATE

adjective
a word that describes a noun

adverb
a word that adds to the meaning of a verb, adjective or another adverb

authoritative
having authority and power

biased
a biased opinion is one based on one viewpoint which doesn't examine the facts fairly

counter viewpoint
an opposing point of view

direct speech
when the words a person has spoken are relayed to the reader exactly, using speech marks

facts
things that are known to have happened or be true

first person
the writer uses 'I' and 'we'

genre
a particular style or type of writing; different fiction genres include thrillers and romance, while non-fiction genres include newspaper articles, letters and speeches

hyperbole
a deliberately exaggerated statement that is not meant to be taken literally

imagery
writing which creates a picture or appeals to other senses; this includes simile, metaphor and personification and the use of vivid verbs, nouns, adjectives and adverbs

metaphor
the use of a word or phrase which describes something by likening it to something else

noun phrase
a group of words that has a noun as its key word

onomatopoeia
words which imitate the sounds they represent

opinions
what someone thinks or believes

prepositional phrase
a word or phrase used with a noun or pronoun to show place, position, time or means, for example, *in a moment*, *far beneath*

prose
writing or speech that is not in verse

pseudonym
a false name

rhetorical question
a question asked for dramatic effect and not intended to get an answer

rule of three
(also called 'tricolon') linking three points or features for impact

second person
addressing the reader as 'you'

sentence forms
sentence types (that is, statement, question, command, exclamation) and sentence structures (that is, simple, minor, multi-clause)

setting
the place in which something is set

simile
a comparison where one thing is compared to another using the words *like* or *as*

synopsis
summary

tense
the tense of the verb tells you when the action of the verb takes place (present, past or future)

tone
a manner of expression in speech or writing

unbiased
impartial, not favouring one side more than the other

verb
a word that identifies actions, thoughts, feelings or the state of being